Olena Martynenko

Quality Management

Afif Hossain
Olena Martynenko

Quality Management

Quality improvement strategies based on brand management, standards, innovation and CSR practices. The Case of LEGO

LAP LAMBERT Academic Publishing

Impressum/Imprint (nur für Deutschland/only for Germany)
Bibliografische Information der Deutschen Nationalbibliothek: Die Deutsche Nationalbibliothek verzeichnet diese Publikation in der Deutschen Nationalbibliografie; detaillierte bibliografische Daten sind im Internet über http://dnb.d-nb.de abrufbar.
Alle in diesem Buch genannten Marken und Produktnamen unterliegen warenzeichen-, marken- oder patentrechtlichem Schutz bzw. sind Warenzeichen oder eingetragene Warenzeichen der jeweiligen Inhaber. Die Wiedergabe von Marken, Produktnamen, Gebrauchsnamen, Handelsnamen, Warenbezeichnungen u.s.w. in diesem Werk berechtigt auch ohne besondere Kennzeichnung nicht zu der Annahme, dass solche Namen im Sinne der Warenzeichen- und Markenschutzgesetzgebung als frei zu betrachten wären und daher von jedermann benutzt werden dürften.

Coverbild: www.ingimage.com

Verlag: LAP LAMBERT Academic Publishing GmbH & Co. KG
Heinrich-Böcking-Str. 6-8, 66121 Saarbrücken, Deutschland
Telefon +49 681 3720-310, Telefax +49 681 3720-3109
Email: info@lap-publishing.com

Herstellung in Deutschland:
Schaltungsdienst Lange o.H.G., Berlin
Books on Demand GmbH, Norderstedt
Reha GmbH, Saarbrücken
Amazon Distribution GmbH, Leipzig
ISBN: 978-3-8484-0554-1

Imprint (only for USA, GB)
Bibliographic information published by the Deutsche Nationalbibliothek: The Deutsche Nationalbibliothek lists this publication in the Deutsche Nationalbibliografie; detailed bibliographic data are available in the Internet at http://dnb.d-nb.de.
Any brand names and product names mentioned in this book are subject to trademark, brand or patent protection and are trademarks or registered trademarks of their respective holders. The use of brand names, product names, common names, trade names, product descriptions etc. even without a particular marking in this works is in no way to be construed to mean that such names may be regarded as unrestricted in respect of trademark and brand protection legislation and could thus be used by anyone.

Cover image: www.ingimage.com

Publisher: LAP LAMBERT Academic Publishing GmbH & Co. KG
Heinrich-Böcking-Str. 6-8, 66121 Saarbrücken, Germany
Phone +49 681 3720-310, Fax +49 681 3720-3109
Email: info@lap-publishing.com

Printed in the U.S.A.
Printed in the U.K. by (see last page)
ISBN: 978-3-8484-0554-1

Acknowledgement

We would also like to thank our families, friends and colleagues for their help and support while writing this book.

Finally, we would like to show our gratitude to the Swedish Government and Karlstad University for giving us an opportunity to do our research in such a peaceful environment.

February 24th, 2012.   Afif Hossain

Karlstad Business School   Olena Martynenko

Preface

In the last decades quality became an interesting hot spot for discussion globally and Quality management has been reckoned as the prime mover for enhanced business performance (Corbett et al., 1998). This increased interest in the quality and quality improvement opened the doors for a new theoretical thinking to emerge; theories concentrating mainly on quality and the way to manage quality. These ideas and principles resulted in what is called nowadays Total Quality Management (TQM).

Through quality management the business firms are striving for innovation and continuous improvement to gain competitive advantage. Also, due to the recent shift from the shareholder view to the stakeholder view many organizations are adopting CSR practices in their management system. Further, the present boom in the service industry and growing serviciczation process in manufacturing industry enables us to observe these facts from a Service-Dominant view. Since, service dominant logic facilitates to examine the phenomenon in a more logical manner in terms of defining concepts like value creation or customer co-creation. Also, the concept of Brand Management needs to be reconsidered in this above mentioned view.

This research paper will enable us to realize how the core values can create value for the company and how it can be embedded in the culture of a company thorough the practice of *CSR*. Moreover, we will try to see how stakeholders' dialogue can be managed through proper *Brand Management*. In addition, the research aims is to find out how the customer co-produces value for the organization as part of *service innovation* besides technical innovation. Finally, the paper has examined how all these existing business concepts drive the company towards a sustainable business.

The study proves that behind all considered concepts in this paper, there are some similar components and actors. If we visualize stakeholder as the centre of the TQM then we will realize how closely CSR, Service Innovation and Brand management are linked to the concept of TQM. And in case of LEGO this link definitely gears the company towards sustainable development. Finally, this phenomenon is easier to explain with the help of Total Responsibility Management (TRM) since it considers stakeholder as the center of doing business.

Key words: Total quality management (TQM), Total responsibility management (TRM), Corporate social responsibility (CSR), Service innovation, Brand management, Service dominant logic, Value creation, Customer co-creation, Sustainable development.

Table of Contents

List of Figures

4

List of Tables

Acronym and Abbreviations

CSR	Corporate Social Responsibility
DKK	Danish Kroner
EHS	Environmental, health and safety
EMS	Environmental management system
ESG	Environmental Social Governance
GRI	Global reporting initiative
ISO	International standard organization
NGO	Non government organization
SD	Service Dominant
SPM	Sustainability performance
TBL	measurement
TQM	Triple bottom line
TRM	Total quality Management
	Total responsibility management

1. Introduction

In the last decades quality became an interesting hot spot for discussion especially in the western world. The Japanese industry achieved a lot of success and managed to gain a competitive edge due to their successful focus on quality and quality related issues (Bergman & Klefsjö, 2003). The quest for quality improvement has become a highly desirable objective in today's intensely competitive global market-place. Quality management has been reckoned as the prime mover for enhanced business performance (Corbett et al., 1998). This increased interest in the quality and quality improvement opened the doors for a new theoretical thinking to emerge; theories concentrating mainly on quality and the way to manage quality. These ideas and principles resulted is what is called nowadays Total Quality Management (TQM).

Through quality management the business firms are striving for innovation and continuous improvement to gain competitive advantage. Also, due to the recent shift from the shareholder view to the stakeholder view many organizations are adopting CSR practices in their management system. Further, the present boom in the service industry and growing serviciczation process in manufacturing industry enables us to observe these facts from a Service-Dominant view. Since, service dominant logic facilitates to examine the phenomenon in a more logical manner in terms of defining concepts like value creation or customer co-creation. Also, the concept of Brand Management needs to be reconsidered in this above mentioned view.

Further, the world is now becoming further more complex than before. The future leader, politicians, CEO's also the stakeholders, needs to understand the complexity of

this global system in which we are living. Since our each and every step affects the future of the world. This enforces the business organizations to behave in a responsible way. Therefore, concepts like total responsibility management (TRM) is also gaining more attention (Waddock et al 2002). As researchers of business administration and social sciences our aim will be to extract the core values that will facilitate organizations to become successful and sustainable.

1.1. Research statement

Focusing on the quality management system of LEGO we will study three other concepts in parallel - these are CSR, Service innovation and Brand Management. We have chosen the case of LEGO since it is one of the leading toy manufacturing company in the world that recovered from major losses in the recent past. The researchers will conduct a longitudinal and explorative study to find out the links between the quality improvements strategies of LEGO based on different quality standards and investigate how it is linked with the company's service innovation process, brand management and CSR practices. Further, we will try to find out whether the links facilitate LEGO on its way to become a sustainable business. We will also figure out the resemblance between TQM and TRM in our research. Finally, we will observe the phenomenon from a service dominant view rather than goods dominant view.

1.2. Purpose of the study

The finding of this research will help to understand the complexity of a quality management system. Further, it will also enable to realize how the core values can create value for the company and how it can be embedded in the culture of a company thorough the practice of *CSR*. Moreover, we will try to see how stakeholders' dialogue can be managed through proper *Brand Management*. In addition, the research aims is to find out how the customer co-produces value for the organization as part of *service innovation* besides technical innovation. Finally, we want to see how all these existing business concepts drive the company towards a sustainable business. We believe the findings of this research will contribute to building a Total Quality Society (Bergman & Klefsjö, 2010) by emphasizing not only the customers and continuous improvement of the process management but also by the way of creating awareness among the stakeholders regarding the quality and smoothly gearing towards a continuously improving society.

1.3. Research Question

1. What is the relationship between QM, CSR, SI and Branding as quality improvement strategies in LEGO?

2. How does this link help to lead the company towards Sustainable Business?

1.4. Research outline

Chapter 1   The first chapter is the **Introduction,** which will enable the reader to get a background of the research. Further, the purpose and research questions are presented in this chapter

Chapter 2   The second chapter illustrates the **Methodology** that was developed for the research. Here we follow a realistic view of the problem. This research will be a qualitative one and will follow deductive method. Further, we will follow a single case study design.

Chapter 3   The Third chapter will develop a **theoretical and conceptual framework** for the reader. This will help to develop a better understanding of empirical study and analysis of the data

Chapter 4   In this section we will give an impression our case that is **LEGO**. It will include a background our **Empirical Study, Analysis** of the collected data concluded with a critical **Evaluation** by the authors.

Chapter 5   In the final chapter we summarize the whole research followed by the **Findings** and concluded with some **Recommendations**

2. Methodology

2.1. Research Philosophy

The main objective of a research work is to re-generate knowledge in a specific area. The first step to carry out a research is to learn about the research philosophy. Since, it contains essential assumptions on how we observe the world (Saunders et al, 2009). Being management and business researchers we need to develop awareness of the philosophical commitments that we will make in our way to select a research strategy, because it does not only influences what we perceive but also on the way how we are examining the case (Johnson and Clark, 2006 cited in Saunders et al 2009). Further, it is not only essential that a research has to be philosophically motivated, but also it is important to know how the researchers reflects on their own philosophical choices and defend these preference alongside the alternative that could have adopted (Saunders et al, 2009). In this chapter we have explained which philosophical approach we have chosen for our research and how it motivated us to define the research strategy.

First of all, the researchers need to clarify the ontological and epistemological orientation of this research paper. Here, ontology refers to the philosophical belief system that deals with the nature of the reality (Saunders et al, 2009). Further, Ontology raises questions on how the researchers draw the assumptions regarding the way how the world operates. Generally, the ontological position can be explained from two stances, these are *Objectivism* and *Subjectivism* (Saunders et al, 2009). Here, objectivism is an ontological position that refers that social phenomenon and its meanings exists and it is independent to social actors. (Bryman & Bell, 2007). On the other hand, subjectivism is an ontological position that is also referred as *constructionism or social constructionism,* states that social phenomena are developed from perceptions and consequent actions of social actors and at the same time these social phenomena are continuously revised (Saunders et al, 2009). This research is related to stakeholders' perspective and it develops a subjective way of doing business. Further, the findings of the research will be drawn from theoretical abstraction; therefore the researchers tend to be more subjectivists and less objectivists (Hossain & Neng, 2010).

Similarly, proper understanding of epistemology enables a researcher select the most suitable research philosophy. Since, epistemology decides what can be considered as acceptable knowledge in certain discipline (Bryman & Bell, 2007). In this regard, the two extreme philosophies are *positivism* and *interpretivism*. Positivism is an epistemological position where the researcher acts as a natural scientist and emphasizes on facts. Generally in this orientation first a hypothesis is developed which is later on tested and confirmed. Also, this kind of research is objective in nature

(Bryman & Bell, 2007). However, in this manner 'the rich insights into the complex world is lost if such complexity is reduced to mere law-like generalizations' (Saunders et al., 2009). In the contrast interpretivism is more linked to phenomenology. In this orientation, phenomenology denotes the approach, through which a human being tries to make sense of the world that surrounds him (Saunders et al., 2009). Further according to interpretivism the fundamentals of social science (i.e. people and their institutions) are quite different from the fundamentals of natural science (Bryman & Bell, 2003). Hence, it is important for the researchers to understand the basics of social action, which is sometimes difficult to notice form a positivist point of view.

Realism is another philosophy that lies in between these two extremes. Realism is a different kind of philosophy which is to some extent similar to positivism (Saunders et al, 2009). Among two kinds of realism, the first type is 'direct realism' which simply denotes that we experience the world through our senses, in other words what we see is what we get (Saunders et al, 2009. p. 114). On the other hand, the second type 'critical realism' argues that the experience that we perceive using our senses can be sometimes misleading, that's why there is a necessity for mental processing after we sense something, in other words reason critically (Saunders et al, 2009). Further, Bryman and Bell (2007) claims critical realism has two implications. Firstly, researcher with a positivist view believes that the researcher's conceptualization of reality directly reflects the reality. In contrast, the realist considers that the researcher's conceptualization is a simple way of knowing the reality. The second implication states that researchers with a critical realist view feels comfortable with theoretical explanations which are sometimes not directly linked to what we observe. (Hossain & Neng, 2010).

Therefore it is evident that simply a positivist or interpretivist approach might not work in case of this research. Hence, our research philosophy is inspired by realism, inclined towards a subjective view of reality. To be more specific we are taking a critical realist approach since the findings of our research greatly support the theoretical framework that we have developed for this research. Besides, Saunders et al. (2009) states that the critical realism is very much appropriate for multi-level (e.g. at the level of individual, group or organization) studies in connection to business and management research (Hossain & Neng, 2010).

In our research we use the research onion recommended by Saunders et al (2009) to show the preference of philosophy and approach of our research.

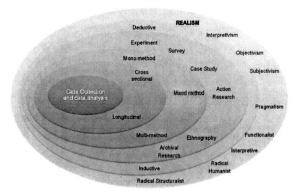

Figure 1: The Research Onion (Saunders et al, 2009)

2.2. Research Approach

2.2.1. Deductive vs Inductive Approach

The question about the application of deductive or inductive approach comes based on several discussions that are contextualized by authors using different aspects. Thus, there is a suggestion that deductive approach is relevant under the condition of the array of theoretical framework on the research topic, whereas new subject and topic with lack of existing theories is a matter of inductively conducted research (Saunders, 2009).

The other aspect that authors Bryman A., Saunders, M., Ghauri P. suggest is that there is interrelationship of deductive and inductive approach with either quantitative or qualitative research. They emphasized deductive approach is usually associated with quantitative research and inductive strategy of linking data and theory is often dealing with qualitative research. However, authors also noted there could be exceptions to the rule.

But the most common view underlies "in the nature of the relationship between theory and research" (Bryman & Bell, 2007, p.11). With deductive approach findings is the outcome of theoretical knowledge where general theory leads to specific reasoning and findings, while inductive is the reverse process with the theoretical conclusions drawn from the collected empirical data.

Saunders et al (2009) also stresses that there is a time span consideration and stated that "deductive research can be quicker to proceed while inductive research can be protracted" (p.126).

Summarizing, we defined that our research is deductive-based one. We are convinced that existing relevant theories are to guide us to make observations and come up with findings on our research topic. Although it was discussed that qualitative research (that is our case) goes along with the inductive approach we still consider it to be deductive, which probably is an exception to the rule that also Bryman and Bell (2007) mentioned. To this as it was stated in Bryman and Bell (2007) and Ghauri (2010) both deductive and inductive approaches cannot be always used pure and may contain elements of each other.

2.3. Research strategy

Research strategy is a general orientation of how the researcher will conduct the research. (Bryman & Bell, 2007). Generally, academic researchers divide research strategy into two different cluster: quantitative and qualitative research (Saunders et al. 2009; Bryman & Bell, 2007).

By definition, qualitative research refers to a strategy that gives more emphasis on words rather than quantification in data collection and analysis. In contrast, quantitative research usually gives more importance on quantification in the collection and analysis of data. Moreover, the common features of qualitative research are, it is inductive, constructive and interpretive. On the other hand quantitative research strategy is deductive, objective and incorporated with natural science (Bryman & Bell, 2007). However, researchers are not obligated to follow all these features while choosing a research strategy.

Though Bryman & Bell (2007) say that the main difference between qualitative and quantitative research is that quantitative researchers use measurement and qualitative researches do not. While, Ghauri and Gronhaug, (2010) argue that the basic difference between qualitative is not about the 'quality' but of procedure. Also, these research strategies are not simply a question of quantification, but also a reflection of different perception of knowledge and research goal. (Ghauri & Gronhaug, 2010). The following table next page gives us a comprehensive view of a quantitative and qualitative research style.

Qualitative research is very much suitable when new theoretical proposition or managerial action is required, but the researcher is not fully aware of the details of the phenomena (Lee, 1999). This view is in line with Ghauri and Gronhaug (2010) who hold that qualitative methods are more appropriate when the objectives of the study require in-depth insight into a phenomenon. Furthermore, Merriam (1998), states that a qualitative approach will enable them to get an overall picture of the issue at hand.

Table 1: Quantitative versus Qualitative style

Quantitative style	Qualitative style
Measure objective facts	Construct social reality, cultural meaning
Focus on variables	Focus on interactive process and events
Reliability is key	Authenticity is key
Value free	Values are present and explicit
Independent of context	Situational constrained
Many cases, subjects	Few cases, subjects
Statistical analysis	Thematic analysis
Researcher is detached	Researcher is involved

Source: Newman W. L (1998) Social Research Methods: Qualitative and quantitative approaches, 3rd edition, Pearson Education, Inc, USA.

In this paper besides qualitative data we have also used quantitative data to cross check the findings of the research which is also known as triangulation method. However, triangulation does not necessarily always mean that it is a combination of qualitative and quantitative research. It can also take place within a qualitative research (Bryman & Bell, 2003). The data extracted from the annual reports of LEGO were quantitative in nature, nevertheless we used it to cross check the qualitative findings of the paper.

Finally, in this paper we have to examine if there is any link between quality improvements strategies of LEGO based on different quality management standards and concepts in relation to innovation and their CSR practices. We believe because of the nature of the study and objective, qualitative research strategy will be more suitable for us.

2.4. Research Design

2.4.1. Case study

The case study as a research design is becoming widely used in management research (Gummesson, 1995). Moreover, "case studies are found in psychology, sociology, political science and even in economics, in which the structure of a given industry or the economy may be investigated by using the case study" (Yin, 2003, p. 1). Ghauri and Gronhaug (2010) provided definition of case study concept that best describes our understanding and project idea by stating that "case study is a description of management situation involving data collection through verbal resources, personal interviews and observation as primary data sources as well as data collection from financial reports, archives, budget and operating statements".

Yin (2003) introduced four types of case study designs based on 2X2 matrix (see Figure 2). The first pair includes single-case and multiple-case study designs. Single-case study is analogous to single experiment and can encompass one of 5 rationales to go for it: critical case, an extreme case, representative case, revelatory case and longitudinal case (Yin, 2003). Our case study is a single-case study with rationale of longitudinal case. Bryman (2003. p. 64) featured "that this type of case is concerned with how the situation changes over the time". Indeed, our research deals with the single company that was an object of investigation within the years. Coming back to some earlier made observations we will further integrate new theories and work out new findings.

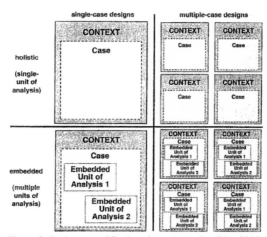

Figure 2: Basic types of Designs for case studies (Yin, 2003)

The other case study designs serve to get holistic or embedded view. With holistic view "detailed observation enable us to study many different aspects, examine them in relation to each other, view the process within its total environment" (Gummesson, 1995, p.76). Whereas, the embedded may involve several units of analysis those are the parts of a one case. With our research we aim to get a holistic view, thus to get entire understanding of the related processes and practices within the one organization.

2.4.2. Data collection

Data collection is a hard and complex work while doing case study and it is because of the absence of routine formulas and routinized processes in this type of research (Yin, 2003). Special skills are also required from researcher to be able to analyze, be tolerant and flexible and be ready to face difficulties while gathering data. Yin (2003) states that even though case study does have some formal plan "the information that may become relevant to a case study is not readily predictable" (p.59).

The great part of our work is related to the identification of theory being studied and the interpretation of it projecting to the data being collected. The most important part is to be able to answer research questions with the help of theory and data with probable deviation if some new findings are being recognized during the research.

2.4.3. Access to data

Data collection always faces difficulty with the preliminary stage and namely *access to data*. Bryman & Bell (2003, p.448) emphasizes that "gaining access is often fraught with difficulties". Therefore, there are a number of access strategies or tactics using formal and informal ways, developing contacts, negotiating (Bryman & Bell, 2003). It is essential to mention that only physical access cannot assure the accuracy and relevancy of data to a study. Saunders (2009) differentiates between *physical access* to the organization that is formally granted through management and *cognitive access* specifying that except entering it is important to be able to choose the right sample of participants who can provide with the data relevant to answer research questions and objectives.

Our research is a longitudinal case study based on a LEGO Company. There have been several studies carried out in a past that gave us sources of earlier secondary data. Moreover, researchers of Service Research Center of Karlstad University have been communicating with the company management and cooperating on the series of issues. So, this helps us to get some secondary data from the company's management.

Literature review and secondary data are the sources that are used to explore and consequently answer research question. Bryman and Bell (2003) specified that literature review is not simply a matter of reproducing theories and opinions of the scholars, but also ability to interpret what they have written (p.95).

However, we admit that thorough study of the existing literature and articles has been leading us along the way towards amending the research question. Discovering new concepts, theories and already studied areas on the research topic generated our interest to find out more and investigate links within the studied subject that got a response in modified research questions. We came to the final formulation of our research question as follow:

- What is the relationship between QM, CSR, SI and Branding as quality improvement strategies in LEGO?
- How does this link help to lead the company towards Sustainable Business?

Moreover, to define boundaries of subject, it is essential not to get away from the research topic.

Usage of *secondary data* will give us a base for reviewing what has been already published. Saunders et al (2009) cited that "secondary data include both raw data and published summaries" (p. 256). Bryman and Bell (2003) pointed out that in case study research "documents can be used to build up a description of the organization and its history because they can give some insights into the past managerial decisions and actions" (p. 566). We are going to use documented secondary data which include written documents in form of reports (Sustainability Reports, CSR Reports), archive documents on company operations (Annual Reports) and other documents (interview with CEO, correspondence) that can be relevant to the case.

To this, multiple-source secondary data survey will be applied. The data can be extracted from several surveys or from the same that has been repeated thus serving to get time series of data over a long period to undertake longitudinal case study (Saunders et al., 2009). Company documents can also provide series of data based on reports over different time spans.

2.4.4. Validity & Reliability

Quality of research can be judged through certain criteria. Researchers mainly use different kind of *validity* and *reliability* measurements to make sure the quality of research. In case of this research we have used numerous tactics in different stage of the research (Bryman & Bell, 2007). In line with this view Yin (2003) mentions "design works actually continue beyond the initial design plans"(p35).

Validity: According to Bryman and Bell (2007) validity in a business research represents the integrity of the findings of a research. Yin (2003) proposes four kinds of test that are normally applied in business research to guarantee the quality of a research. These are the following-

Construct Validity: is the first test that is conducted in the data collection and composition phase. Through this test the researchers establishes operational measures of the concepts that will be studied. To fulfill the requirement of this test, first we decided to study the theories individually. Subsequently we selected some relevant common measures to find out the links in between the collected data and chosen theories. We used *multiple source of evidence* as a tactic in our data collection process.

17

For example, we have collected articles from various authentic data bases to study the theories and also we have gone through different sources to collect second data for our case.

Internal validity: is the second test that is performed in the data analysis phase which is usually used in causal and explanatory case studies not suitable for exploratory studies. Since our research is an exploratory study so we didn't undertake this test to check the internal validity of the research. However, we have related the empirical study on the company LEGO with the theoretical and conceptual frame that ensures the internal validity of our research (Bryman & Bell, 2007).

External validity: this test is connected to research design. External validity deals with extent to which the results of the research can be generalized. Nevertheless, it is hard to ensure the external validity of a research, particularly for single case study. To overcome this problem we have supported our case with a well structured theoretical base.

Reliability: is the last test takes place in the data collection phase. Reliability in a research measures the degree, to which data collection analysis procedures or techniques deliver the same results no matter how many times it is applied (Saunders et al, 2009; Bryman & Bell, 2007; Ghauri & Gronhaug, 2010). The purpose of reliability in a case study is to repeat the same study more than one time to check whether findings and conclusions of the research are always same (Yin, 2003). The goal of reliability is not to repeat the same research again but to minimize the biasness and errors in a research. In this research we have used previous studies that have been carried out on LEGO to strengthen reliability of the findings of our case study.

2.5. Ethical considerations:

Ethics in research denotes the appropriateness of the researcher's action in relation to the rights of the people who turn out to be the subject of a research or those who are affected by it. Further, research ethics is also related to how we generate research question, design research strategy, get access to data, interpret and analyze those data, finally sum up our findings in a moral and responsible way (Saunders et at 2010). In this sense ethics in research is subject to the soundness of research methodology and moral defensibility for the people who are subject to research.

The ethical principles in a research can be divided in four different (Bryman & Bell, 2007). These includes –

Harm to participants: if confidentiality or anonymity is requested by the participants of the research then we have honor it. We have used interviews and speech of LEGO officials that were shared by the company itself for its stakeholders in different websites. So in our case anonymity and confidentiality was not required.

Lack of informed consent: The participant in a research has the right to be fully aware of the research process. Since the secondary data that we used for the research were taken from open sources where the participants shared their identity and opinion themselves so consent of the participants were not required.

Invasion of privacy: Often participants refuse to answer the questions in an interview. These refusals are usually based on a felling of certain question that might be sensitive for the participant and also invade his/her privacy. Since, the people who are subject to our research have disclosed their identity in public willingly, so we believe we are not invading their privacy.

Deception: takes place when the researcher misrepresents their research other than what it is. This is subject to soundness of the methodology that we will use. We have already clarified our research philosophy and research strategy elaborately to prove the appropriateness of our research

3. Theoretical and Conceptual framework

3.1. The notion of quality

The term 'quality' has been derived from the Latin word 'qualitas' means 'of what' was first used by Cieroan roman narrator and politician lived in 106-46 BC (Bergman & Klefsjö, 2003) In general, the word quality means to standardize something in comparison to some other similar kind of things or to express a distinct attribute of something. However, in the last couple of decades in the business world this word has gained significant importance and has acquired a broader meaning. Gurus of quality have defined quality from different perspectives. Among them Joseph Juran's (1951) defined quality from a customer centric view stating *"Fitness for use"*. Further Juran breaks down the concept of quality into two separate elements, first the product has to be defected less and second is that it should have the properties to fulfill customer needs, in other words it should create value for the customers. Whereas, Edward Deming's (1986) definition of quality *"Quality should be aimed at the needs of customer, present and future"*, emphasized that today's customer will be tomorrow's customer. However, the Japanese author Genichi Taguchi (Taguchi & Wu, 1979) has defined quality as *"The lack of quality is the losses a product imparts from the society from the time the product is shipped"*. Taguchi's definition of quality has broader meaning where he has connected not only the customers but also those who are not directly consuming the product, means the stakeholders. Bergman & Klefsjö (2003) has stated that this definition of Taguchi is strongly related to concepts like CSR, Sustainable Development and Sustainable society. Furthermore, it shows the concern about the environmental problems. Another broad definition is given by Bergam and Klefsjö, (2010) as they stated that *"The quality of a product is its ability to satisfy, or preferably exceed the needs and expectations of the customers"* (p.24). Which implies that the product offered to the customer is not enough, instead we need to innovate something that will exceed their expectations.

Here we feel the necessity to define the concept of customer as well. One narrow view that has been used to define customer concept in ISO 9000 is "Organization or person who receives a product. However Bergman and Klefsjö (2010) has defined customer from a broader view. According to them customers are "those we want to create value for". Customers can be any people or organization for whom the main business organization is creating value. Here the value is linked to value chain of the business organization not the financial chain. Furthermore, they have included the future generations as well, who might be affected by the present activities of the business organization as well. This broader concept of customer is in line with Jurans (1988) where he defines customer as "anyone who is affected by the product or by the process used to produce the product. Another idea proposed by Noraman (2001) (cited in Bergman and Klefsjö 2003) was that he considered customer as a co-producer of value creating network. This implies that customer co-creates value for the products. This view is closely linked to service dominant logic that we will discuss in the following chapters.

Further drawing from Garvin's (1984) discussion we can perceive five approaches of quality concepts. These are transcendent, product-based, user-based, manufacturing based and value based perspective. According to the *transcendent* perspective quality cannot be measured precisely and can only be identified when it is experienced; 'quality lies in the eye of the beholder'. In contrast, the *product-based* view implies that quality can be measured exactly and is measured through the desirable characteristics a product possesses. Garvin states, the higher the quality the higher the cost and the quality is objective intrinsic attribute of the product moreover it can't be judged by the users of buyers. Whereas, *user-based* approach supports the idea that customer is the evaluator of quality. Further, *manufacturing-based* approach refers to the execution of tolerance and prerequisites in production. Here quality is mainly focuses on technical innovation. Lastly, value-based approach quality is linked to the price and cost of the product. The high quality product possesses higher value at a preferable price or performance at a suitable cost. Finally Garvin (1984) states an organization may need to adopt more than one approach of quality concepts for different departments of the organization as each concept is related to a specific sector or part of the organization. Some are internal and related to production, operation, or cost, others are more customer focus and external.

3.2. TQM as a management system and it's components

A lot of studies specify that Quality Management "is more than unifying objective and mechanism, it is a philosophy, it integrates the entire management of the company" (Grant et al. 1994, p.28). Further Quality management consists of a set of principles for managing a company and the definition of these principles varies among the authors in the literature and probably the most common principle is focus on customer. Quality management conceptualize a firm as a "chain of linked processes whose end point is a customer" (Grant et al. 1994, p.32). However, Quality management (QM) is commonly understood as a management philosophy that drives the company towards better maintenance and continuous improvement of all the functions in an organization with an objective to fulfill the growing needs of customer. The concept of Quality management is often referred as total quality management (TQM) and also exceeds quality standards such as ISO 9001 (Molina-Azorín et al, 2009). By the end of 1980's TQM has become an imperative for most of the major corporations (Waddock, 2004).

Bergman and Klefsjö (2003) defined Total Quality Management as *"a constant endeavor to fulfill, and preferably exceed, customer needs and expectations at the lowest cost, by continuous improvement work, to which all involved are committed, focusing on the processes in the organization"* (p.34).

According to Hellsten & Klefsjö (2000) the concept of TQM is generally understood as some form of "management philosophy" based on a number of core values such as customer focus, continuous improvement, process orientation, everybody's commitment, fast response, result orientation and learn from others. These core values are similar to the values that are represented as the cornerstones of TQM by Bergman and Klefsjö (2003). These cornerstones are four cornerstones that are self explanatory; *base decisions on facts, focus on processes, improve continuously* and *let everyone be committed*. These four cornerstones all intertwine with the focus on customers because that's the important goal that these corner stone are focusing on. Around all these cornerstones the committed leadership role comes wrapping them all together and insuring their efficient and successful implementation. Motwani (2001) has defined TQM as a house where the foundation is *top management commitment* and the pillars of this house will be *employees training and empowerment, quality measurement and benchmarking, process management and customer involvement and satisfaction.* Lastly, when the pillars will be in place the organizations can focus into *supplier quality management* and *product design.* The discussion clarifies that management plays the most important role in quality management. Also, integration of the suppliers into the quality system is vital step.

Top Management Commitment

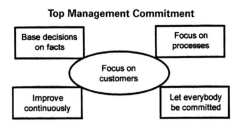

Figure 3: The corner stone's of TQM (Bergman & Klefsjö, 2003)

TQM is often compared with different quality awards like Malcolm Baldrige National Awards, European Quality Award and Swedish Quality Award. The core values of these awards are namely referred as dimensions, cornerstone, elements or principles. Even though the number of the core values differs in these quality awards but the basic core values/cornerstones of TQM are noticeable almost in all these awards.

Table 2: Core Values of Quality Awards

Malcom Baldrige National Quality Award	European Quality Award	The Swedish Quality Award
Customer-driven quality	Results orientation	Customer orientation
Leadership	Customer focus	Committed leadership
Continuous improvement and learning	Leadership and consistency of purpose	Participation by everyone
Valuing employees	Management by processes and facts	Competence development
Fast response		Long-range perspective
Design quality and prevention	People development and involvement	Public responsibility
Long-range view of the future	Partnership development	Process orientation
Management by fact	Public responsibility	Prevention
Partnership development		Continuous Improvement
Public responsibility and citizenship		Learning from others
Result focus		Faster response
		Management by facts
		Partnership

Source: (Hellsten & Klefsjö, 2000).

However, TQM is more than core values. Core value is just a component of TQM that is the foundation of the culture of the organization. The other two components are technique and tools. Here techniques guide the organization to realize its core values whereas the tools are instruments that sometimes use statistical methods to analyze the data. Hence, we see a culture in an organization is developed based on the core values which is the first step. Then to attain and maintain the culture the core values constantly need to be supported by appropriate technique and tools. These three components are interdependent. (Hellsten & Klefsjö, 2000). Means TQM can be treated as a management system where the core values are supported by the techniques and tool and are aimed at increasing the internal and external customer satisfaction with minimum amount of resources.

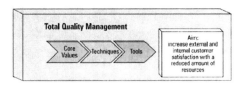

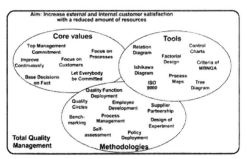

Figure 4: Role of Core Value, Technique and Tool (Hellsten & Klefsjö, 2000)

However, some realize TQM to be necessary for gaining competitive advantage, other think it is nothing but just a vague concept and this creates confusion about the term TQM. One reason behind this is that the quality Gurus didn't like the term TQM. Deming was against using the term TQM and referred it as a buzz word. Also, Juran stated that TQM consist of the principles of Baldrige Award and refused to use it. Further, confusion arises with term TQM because of the existence of similar concept like Total Quality Improvement, Companywide control, strategic quality management. The differences in between these concepts are not clear that leads to confusion. The third reason is alarming as there are many vague definition of TQM (Hellsten & Klefsjö, 2000).

3.3. Quality Management as competitive advantage

Improved quality undoubtedly affects the success and prosperity of any organization in many ways. Some examples of the advantages from improved quality can be (Bergman & Klefsjö, 2003):

1. More satisfied and loyal customers
2. Lower employee turnover
3. Stronger market posititon
4. Shorter lead times
5. Opportunities for capital release
6. Reduced costs due to waste and rework
7. Higher productivity

In many ways, improved quality can result in improved profitability. As per Bergman and Klefsjö, by enhancing the internal quality, it is possible to drastically minimize the need for intermediate stock and reserves. So that, high quality is a pre-requisite for Just-In-Time (JIT) approaches. They also said that, it is possible to use a reduction of buffer stocks and other reserves to bring quality problem into the light. Once this have been eliminated, further storage reduction can be possible which will in turn lead to improved quality and lower storage cost.

According to Molina-Azorín et al (2009) quality management increases customer satisfaction and improves process with the intention of cost reduction, waste prevention and waste management. This customer centric approach and the approach to cost reduction ultimately lead to strategy for cost leadership.

Sureshchandar et al (2002) mentioned that, "much has been written about the philosophy of total quality management (TQM)/total quality service (TQS) and its ability to result in competitive success. Several researchers have repeatedly underlined the significance of quality improvement initiatives in resulting in a sustainable competitive advantage. We find the same opinion from some other researchers also- "many studies have provided ample evidence that quality and all aspects of quality have always scored highly as an important competitive capability" (Corbett, 1994; Kim, 1995, cited in Sureshchandar et al 2002). From their writing, we also find that, in a significant research work, provided valuable insights on the 'soft issues' of TQM. His work explored TQM as a possible source of sustainable competitive advantage and found that certain implicit like behavioral, imperfectly imitable features, like open culture, employee empowerment and executive commitment, are vital for an environment conducive to TQM (Sureshchandar et al 2002). We can say, it takes a lot of efforts to develop a TQM based production system and it will eventually benefit the organizational success for sure.

TQM aims at creating "increased customer satisfaction with a reduced amount of resources" (Bergman & Klefsjö, 2003, p51). This analogy by the authors suggests that TQM have a positive long term effect on the profitability and productivity of the company. They also suggest that TQM will enhance work environment and work developments. Hence, we see this positive relation with quality leads organization ultimately to success in many different ways (Sureshchandar et al., 2002; Molina-Azorín et al, 2009).

25

3.4. Corporate Social Responsibility and its link with Quality Management

The contemporary view of CSR shows a company's dedication toward its social and environmental obligation in order to build a strong relation with its customers and stakeholders (Edvardsson & Enquist, 2009). An ethical company with strong and social and environmental sense shows its concerns for its stakeholders. If a CSR approach in adopted in an organization's practice then the organization might undergo a basic change from its stockholder oriented approach to a social harmony. To achieve this stage the organization has to establish a balance between its shareholders and other stakeholder group (Enquist et al, 2006). Here, the stakeholders include customer, employees, NGO, activist media, suppliers, shareholders and investors. (Waddock et al, 2002). Unfortunately, this means that the companies these days do not meet the requirements of customer and stakeholder in terms of ethical, environmental and social issues that might have a negative impact on the image that in its turn may result in loosing customer.

For the resent time companies are focusing on their core values supported by strong sense of CSR. (Enquist et al, 2006). However, question arises whether there is a business imperative for CSR and can it be taken into account as a core value. Since, many researchers has criticized it for being just a concept for customer eye wash or just for charity gesture to attain profit in the short term. Vogel (2005) says there is no evidence that clearly proves existence of positive link between profitability and responsibility. However, it doesn't necessarily means that there is no business case for CSR. Further, it makes business sense for business organization in particular situation. Afterwards, having made a multiple case study on service oriented firms Enquist et al (2008) proves that CSR can't be seen merely as a charity or 'doing good for doing good' but 'doing good for doing well'. Further the study states that the innovative service based companies are getting a competitive advantage based on triple bottom line thinking. Here, the so called triple bottom line thinking guides the company towards a sustainable business based on economic, social and environmental issues (Elkington, 1997). This also facilitates to consider CSR as an integral part of service logic.

Now coming to the point whether CSR can be seen within TQM context? McAdam and Leonard (2003) stresses that TQM can be used as a foundation to develop CSR within an organization, since both TQM and CSR leads toward a sustainable development based on environmental protection, social equity and economic growth. Further, they provide a dualistic definition of CSR. Firstly, CSR can be defined as 'ethical anchor'. Here, the ethical anchor refers to legitimate ethics or the ethical behavior that is embedded in our society. Secondly, it can be viewed as an instrument

26

that strengthens the image of the company where achivements of the organizational goals are the main concern. This definition is similar to TQM, since TQM also has a strong ethical focus (Leonard & McAdam, 2003). Further, it aims at achieving organizational goal and success. Moreover, in comparison with the other TQM awards (see table 2) CSR also pays attention to leadership, people, process and it is result oriented. This means CSR can be integrated in the existing TQM model of a company without changing the companies present management system in relation to stakeholder. (Leonard & McAdam, 2003) Thus, the combination of both approaches will guide the organization to avoid irrelevant change and gear the organization towards its quality journey.

Finally, the complexity of the CSR meaning can be used to misguide and mislead stakeholder. CSR practice of an organization can only be promoted in a proper way to stakeholders through maintenance of high level of transparency. Further, transparency is required for measuring quality as well. The transparency can be gained through internationally accepted reporting guidelines that are subject of 'corporate governance'. This raises the question whether a convergence is possible between CSR and Corporate Governance for the sake of good governance that is now stated as 'New Governance' (Gill, 2008) Further, the companies are not always led by the owners, instead they can be is lead by the managers who follow the intention of the owner in other words share holders. And when the managers don't follow the intention of the shareholders it increases risk. Sometimes managers take extra risk to show better performance of the company by manipulating reports, since the satisfaction of the shareholder becomes the central objective for the managers. This enhances the ongoing convergence of the both theories CSR and CG. Bergman & Klefsjö (2003) see this integration to be important for the sustainable development of the company.

3.5. Quality Management to Responsibility Management

There is an ongoing discussion whether TQM should be replaced by Total Responsibility Management (TRM). Waddock and Bodwell (2004) defined responsibility management "sets a fairly standard of performance with respect to the relationship that a company develops with its stakeholders through its strategies and operating practices"(p. 28). As we have seen from the previous discussion that quality management focuses on the customer needs and tries to exceed them to gain their loyalty. Similarly, responsibility deals with the demand and expectation of the stakeholders including the customer and employees, by mutual engagement and dialogue with the stakeholders through 'stakeholder engagement' or 'stakeholder dialogue' (Waddock & Bodwell, 2004, Waddock et al 2002). This means the customer is the center of TQM, whereas stakeholder is the center of TRM.

27

Further, pressure is created by the stakeholder and societal groups to develop TRM based system in the corporation. The pressure mainly comes from three major parties. Firstly, the primary stakeholders, such as shareholder, employees, supplier and most important the customers; secondly, the secondary stakeholders this includes NGO's, activist and Government; Thirdly, global standards and principles and reporting guidelines such as UN Global Compact, ISO standards and GRI reporting guidelines aiming on multiple bottom-line rather than one bottom-line (Waddock et al 2002). Here, we can see that TQM focuses more on the primary stakeholder, whereas TRM has to consider all three parties. Therefore, TRM covers a broader group of stakeholders than TQM. However, there is no contradiction in the core value of quality management and responsibility management.

Similarly, like three components for TQM proposed by Hellsten & Klefsjö (2000) (see figure 4) an integrated TRM model has three major approaches. The first approach is *inspiration* that starts with a vision of responsible practice. This vision determines the values or responsibilities that will be the base of the TRM system. Second, approach is *integration* of those responsibilities in a firm's corporate strategy through managing human resource and managing system. Final approach is continuous *innovation and improvement* using indicators, which can measure responsibility and learn from experience with the progress of time. In the last approach high level of transparency and accountability is required. However, alike quality it is difficult to measure responsibility. Yet, with the advancement of social auditing like balance score card or GRI reporting it is possible to measure responsibility, whereas statistical tools are used to measure quality (Waddock & Bodwell, 2004, Waddock et al 2002). We have developed the following table to show the contrast and relationship between TQM components and TRM approaches.

Table 3: Comparison between TQM components and TRM approaches

TQM components	TRM approaches
Core Values	Inspiration process
Based on top management commitment	Responsibility Vision, Values
Focus on process	Leadership Built on Foundational Values
Improve continuously	Stakeholder Engagement
Let everybody be committed	
Focus on customer	
Base decision on fact	
Technique	Integration Processes
Policy deployment	Strategy
Employee development	Human Resource Responsibility
Process management	Integration into Management Systems
Benchmarking, Six Sigma, MBQNA	Responsibility Measurement Systems
Tools	Innovation and improvement process
ISO 9001	Balance scorecard
Process Map	Strategic audit
Control chart, tree diagram	Global reporting initiative
	Holistic performance assessment
Goal: Satisfy internal and external customers	Goal: Satisfy stakeholder and societal group
This table doesn't provide a complete list of TQM components or TRM approaches. Since no one concept or approach is enough to represent the system and also it is subject to continuous change. It is developed to compare the general frame of both TQM and TRM systematic management process	

(Hellsten & Klefsjö,2000 ; Waddock & Bodwell, 2004)

3.6. Sustainable Development through quality improvement

The concept of Sustainable Development (SD) was first introduced in Brundtland commission report that was published in 1987, there sustainable development was defined as "development that meets the need of the present without compromising the ability of future generations to meet their own needs". The Brundland report contains the following principles (Bergman & Klefsjö, 2010):

- A long term perspective
- Continuous improvement
- Integration of environmental, social and economic aspects in the decision making
- Develop new model for growth
- Respect for the ecological systems
- Justice between generations and within generations.

The concept of Sustainable development contains three dimensions. These are economic, environmental and social sustainability (Enquist & Sebhatu, 2007). Here, economic sustainability needs to be argued for a global perspective. In order to stay in the business and to satisfy the customers the company has to go for high quality. On the other hand social sustainability refers to satisfy the stakeholders. For example, by provide the employees with a better physical and psychological work environment through ensuring proper health and safety standards. On global level, deal with human rights, child labor and exploitation of workforce in a positive manner. Finally, environmental sustainability can be ensured by the proper use of energy, showing respect for the natural resources with a long term goal. (Bergman & Klefsjö, 2010). Hence, a CSR philosophy can be adopted towards sustainable development, since CSR covers all the principles of SD.

The shift towards sustainable thinking is encouraging the organizations to adopt triple bottom-line and become more value-driven and responsible (Enquist et.al. 2006). Inspired by the idea of value-based business Sebhatu (2008) developed a sustainability performance measurement (SPM) framework (Table 4) He further related it with the TRM philosophy and integrated it with Post et al.s', (2002) descriptive, instrumental and normative contributions of stakeholder view. Post et al. (2002) *descriptive* highlights not only social and political aspects of an organization, but also emphasizes the humanitarian, ethical and behavioral issues. These are important for the stakeholders and also vital in the long term existence of the company. Whereas, Normative is the consideration of the core values those have to be updated continuously and maintained in the companies through learning process. Finally, *instrumental* deals with the wealth creation process not only emphasizing "rational wealth", but also for the potential threat. (Post et al, 2002 cite in Sebhatu, 2008). We will use the indicators in this framework to measure the performance of LEGO.

Table 4: The Sustainability Performance Measurement Framework

Environment	Performance Measurements	Indicators
Surface/External	Triple Bottom Line - Elkington, 1998	Environmental
		Social
		Economic
Internal	TRM - Leadership	
	Waddock and Bodwell, 2007	Integration (different standards)
	Post et al., 2002	Descriptive/Potential-values
		Normative/Core-values
		Instrumental/Value- creation

(Sebhatu, 2008.p5)

30

3.7. Service Innovation with Service-Dominant perspective

Innovation is quite a new modern word that become popular with the technological progress and quickly developing markets in the growing economy. There is a great concern around innovation across companies, manufacturers, customers. Why does innovation become a necessity, a tool to compete and succeed? What is special about it and what drives innovation process? In this chapter we are going to define and conceptualize innovation process, its components, participants, driving forces. This will help us to encompass a broader view on the existing concepts of innovation, its implications and will help us to find links with other theories raised in research question.

The definition of innovation can be given in the angle of market and as such it is any idea, product, service, which is perceived by customer as being new (New Inventions Success, 2011). There are different types of innovations that are related to the spheres where the innovation can take place and also depending on the participants, business concepts, speed of technological and economical growth. It also depends on customer expectations, needs, demands and knowledge.

3.7.1. Service-Dominant Logic and value co-creation

Talking about innovation process, it's participants, focus on customer and previously mentioned quality perspectives we feel necessity to mention about shifting from Goods-Dominant Logic to Service-Dominant Logic and concept of value creation and co-creation because this generate further process of innovation.

In a chapter about quality we touched the question of 5 quality approaches from Garvin's (1984) perspectives: transcendent, product-based, user-based, manufacturing based and vale-based quality. The common idea in differentiation of them lies in participation or absence of doer/user/evaluator. As we mentioned before that the most common principle of Quality Management is focus on customer, so customer is the one who evaluates. Transcendent, user-based and values-based quality approaches are those that are linked with the users/customers involvement, whereas product-base and manufacturing are more related to product characteristics and production superiority and capacity. While talking about users and customers involvement in quality perspectives we have already proved that they are the direct actors in quality assessments and consumption. Only with the customers involvement the services can be experienced and evaluated. Here we have to describe the concept of Service-Dominant Logic (S-D) and Goods-Dominant Logic (G-D) with their value-in-use and value-in-exchange determinants. This concept got significant attention and a lot of articles are written to support and develop it.

31

The article written by Stephen L. Vargo, Paul P. Maligo and Melissa Archpru Akaka titled "on value and value co-creation: a service system and service logic perspective" has considered service as an application of competencies (knowledge and entities), by one entity for the benefit of another (Vargo & Lusch, 2004). This means value is created collaboratively in interactive configurations of mutual exchange. What the authors refer as service systems. Here, service science is considered as the study of service system and also of the co-creation of value within complex constellation of integrated resources. (Vargo et al, 2008) At this point the authors tired to configure the process of value co-creation and measurement of value in use.

The authors determined Goods-Dominant Logic the one that is based on the value-in-exchange meaning of value where goods usually products of manufacturers and distributed through exchange of goods and money, whereas service-dominant logic is linked to the value-in-use meaning of value and the roles of producer and consumer are not distinct (Vargo et al., 2008). The basic differentiation between S-D Logic and G-D Logic lies in exchange and Vargo et al (2008) defined that in S-D logic the focus is on interactions of operant resources such as knowledge and skills and in G-D Logic there is an exchange of operand resources such as goods that are the subjects to operate or act on. From this perspective "value results from the beneficial application of operant resources, which are sometimes transmitted through operand resources or goods and so values is co-created through combined efforts of employees, customers, other stakeholders" (Vargo et al., 2008, p.148). Furthermore, value is created through the active participation of different service systems engaged in exchange. This is clear that integration and association of various social and economics science disciplines is essential for the better understanding of value and value creation (Vargo et al, 2008).

Value-in-use will not happen until offering is done and experience is gone through by customer. The value of market offering is only defined by the individual customer (Michel et al., 2008). Customer is called co-creator or co-producer of value of services they get. Nice example of IKEA was given by Norman & Ramirez (1993) to show how customers can create value and not just consume it. The company forces the customers to think about value introducing them participation, work-sharing and new experience that will bring value and positive emotions of doing something out of the way.

On a way to discontinuous innovation Michel et al. (2008) noted that this co-creation stipulates that customers can perform several roles: users, buyers and payers; i.e. in case of users it refers to value-in-use, payer is related to value-in-exchange and buyers is a combination of 2 previous roles (p.61). At the perspective of Service-Dominant Logic customers' role is transforming to users' role rather than payers' role with its value-in-exchange concept. Michel et al. (2008) defined innovation as discontinuous innovation and underlined that "discontinuous innovation stresses inclusion of operant resources (skills, knowledge) within an offering or experience in ways that enable the customer to innovate" (p.65). Vargo et al. (2008) also emphasized the tremendous need for service innovations and usage of intangible resources that can raise the quality and effectiveness of services.

Value co-creation brings innovation and evolution within the market. Moreover, it generates new knowledge in the way of doing business. In this way the interdisciplinary exchange of ideas and existing knowledge will increase the understanding of value co-creation. Spohrer et al. (2008) in article "Toward Systematic Service Innovations to Accelerate Co-Creation of Value" mentioned about the systematic innovation and also advocate that service innovation creates changes in the whole service system that is made up of clients and providers co-creating value and which has an impact on the system evolution. Under putting service innovation into being more systematic the authors defined three aspects from which this system can seem to work efficiently: investing in talent, investing in technology and providing superior environment for performance (Spohrer et al, 2008). Investing in talent can be treated almost the same (as was mentioned previously) as knowledge and skills that will allow to offer wide range of services with high level of unique customization, technology creates opportunities towards offering new efficient configurations of services and performance environment is linked to the provider physical environment and employee service and efficiency that effect customer perception of the service. Finally, the authors noted that "service innovations have the potential to impact service productivity, service quality and rates of growth and return for service systems" (Sporer et al., 2008, p. 244).

As we mentioned value co-creation and discontinuous innovation process requires participation of several parties which involve such stakeholders as customers, employees, suppliers and providers. Dedication and commitment of stakeholders can contribute to the overall process that finally leads to the customer satisfaction. These are the touch points with TQM philosophy. Moreover, TQM uses such technique as employee development and process management that also found reflection on the way of creating value for the customer.

3.7.2. Product innovation versus Service innovation

We have figured Service-Dominant Logic and Goods-Dominant Logic perspectives and basic shifts in that area and that value co-creation brings innovation within the markets. Further we have to define nature of product innovation and service

33

innovation and see how value creation and exchange of operant resources and operand resources have place in both cases.

Before coming to the understanding of the product and service innovation notion and differentiation we should first of all emphasize that this differentiation is based on the difference of products and services themselves. By nature services are different from the products and can be characterized by the following key definitions: intangibility, inseparability, variability, perishability and lack of ownership (Lovelock & Wirtz, 2007, p.17). These make services unique and quite difficult in managing their distribution and provision.

One of the major trends of recent years has been the phenomenal growth of services stipulated by the changes in the overall economy and progress, i.e increasing of the service sector of the economy, increasing global competition, governmental policies, social changes, business trends, advances in information technology and internationalization (Lovelock & Wirtz, 2007) . If we take as an example information technology factor we can easily notice in our everyday life that advanced technology really increased the number of services we are getting today (internet for booking tickets, online payment, consultations online, mobile services, etc). The markets became more saturated with products and especially with sophisticated products that require further service, maintenance or training on their implications and operation. "Moreover, as companies find it harder to differentiate their physical products, they increasingly turn to service differentiation, seeking to win and retain customers through delivering superior services" (Kotler et al., 2005). Also, a great part of population in every country is employed in service providing jobs.

Vermeulen and Van der Aa (2003) discussed that intangibility of services affect the development process and make new service development more complex when compared to the developing physical products because developers can not touch, see, feel the new service but at the same time it can appear to be easier since there are no prototypes and major investment in raw materials as in the case of new products development. Heterogeneity doesn't make much difference and can affect in the same extent both new service and product development. Also "the fact that services cannot be stored (perishability feature) doesn't mean that they cannot be developed in advance at the conceptual level" (Vermeulen & Van der Aa, 2003, p.39). Nevertheless, Voss & Zomerdijk (2007) pointed out that service innovation "has proved an elusive area for many reasons including intangibility of services, the heterogeneity of services, much innovation being of processes rather than products and the lack of an identifiable R&D function" and that "technology is being used to change the nature of services (p. 99). Indeed, the technological factor generate the innovation in services. Technology has

34

been becoming as a supportive tool to service innovation i.e. with the help of new advanced technology service area generate more innovative approaches to reach the customers and to introduce more complicated improved service.

The differentiation between product innovation and service innovation is not clear, they are both complement each other and it much more depend on the industry and service areas. Sometimes even modern academic literature doesn't specify what type of innovation it narrates about. This happen due to the fact that nowadays there are no pure products and no pure services, companies try to introduce complex product with services attached. In some academic sources the combination of both manufacturing products and services in the offer and as such as tool for driving innovation is represented differently but with the same meaning. Tether and Howells (2007), for example, noted that the synthesis approach provides the increasing complex and multidimensional character of innovation and this facilitate bundling of services and manufactured goods into "solutions" (p.35). Howells (2004) advocates concept about "service encapsulation" and the combinatorial role of services. He highlights that services "can play intermediary and conduit role in the innovation process" as to the goods and services and that "services encapsulate, or act as "wrappers" to, goods". (Howells, 2004, p.23).

It was said that nowadays product innovation and service innovation doesn't have clear boundaries and this happen due to the deep customization process and shift from Goods-Dominant Logic towards Service-Dominant Logic. Products wrapped in services are developed to exceed customers' expectations and satisfy their needs and the more the customer is demanding and expecting the more companies are trying to innovate, improve and suggest continuously. That's why innovation is not a short-term phenomena. So, this makes us assume that innovation has direct link to the TQM concept. One of the cornerstones of TQM is "improve continuously" and this is the case of service innovation as well. Moreover, continuous innovation and improvement is one of the components of TQM and one of the approaches of TRM. Besides, the other link that the same as TQM concept calls for is that service innovation is focusing on customer.

3.7.3. Drivers of service innovation

Previously we mentioned increase of services provided and the speed of economical development and therefore a lot of companies need to react faster to the markets changes in order to stay competitive and this drives service innovation process. Indeed, Bessant & Davies (2007) specify that "innovation matters significantly to service players and if they don't change their offerings and the ways they create and deliver those then their survival and growth is in question" (p.64). Moreover, innovation process needs to lead to the creation of services that will be unique and difficult to imitate by competitors and followers (Bessant & Davies, 2007, p.91). That means that innovation is steady process that is changing and progressing over the time span.

Bessant and Davies (2007) also figured out 3 up-to-date processes that drive innovation: servicisation, customization and outsourcing (p.88). We consider them as tendencies that push innovation. Growth of services that "encapsulate" manufactured products is the case we already figured out and this also can be featured as servicisation. "Such patterns of manufacturing blurring into services businesses - "servicisation" - are increasingly found and pose significant challenges to the underlying skills base in general and to innovation skills in particular" (Bessant & Davies, 2007, p.88). In this servicisation era the authors arguing about the importance of handling customer insights rather than focusing on pure research and development (R&D) activities. The other tendency is customization process which is characterized by a shift towards creating personal customer service rather than offering standard product with services offerings. This has been long discussed as there is an issue of price tag involved that can entail high cost of customized services. Bessant and Davies (2007) emphasized that "combination of enabling technologies and rising customer expectations has begun to shift this balance and resolve the trade-off between price and customisation" (p.91). And another third tendency is development of outsourcing phenomenon which can be seen in relocation of some functional processes to other companies with purpose of cost reduction and there could be two types defined "transactional" and "strategic" outsourcing (Bessant & Davies, 2007, p.91). Transactional outsourcing is focusing on some standard functional transition while the latter should represent high potential for head companies which outsource some strategic functions which under development can be a "powerful source of service innovation" (Bessant & Davies, 2007, p.91).

These drivers of innovation as customization, servicization and outsourcing tendencies are directly dealing with economical and social issues. The matter of costs and price for customized product are at question. This thinking of companies makes it similar to that of triple bottom line thinking that takes account of economic, social and environmental issues. In this respect such social issue as customer insights is the other driver of service innovation which is mention by Voss and Zomerdijk (2007). The understanding of customer's needs and wants drive the innovation process towards improvement and customer satisfaction. This continuous improvement builds another link of service innovation to quality management concept. Moreover, service innovation has in common some considerations from triple bottom line thinking that ultimately directed to sustainable development.

3.7.4. User innovation

We considered understanding of service innovation from a broader perspective which cannot exist in vacuum and require to be integrated in developed system which include interdisciplinary nature of service, social, business, integrating technology, customer innovations. But we can also have a look at smaller cell of service innovation that happen on the level of customer experience. Service co-creation and value-in-use make customer to be innovator based on his experience as a user.

User innovation has been investigated by Dr. Peter Magnusson who worked on research on user innovation and specifically on actual contribution of end users. He stresses that "there appears to be a trend toward companies involving potential consumers in idea generation with respect to new products and services" (Magnusson, 2009, p. 579) It was also mentioned that special factors for successful user involvement are important among which motivation, user experience and user knowledge of technology.

Magnusson (2009) conceptualized two types of users: ordinary users and lead users. Ordinary users are those that on average don't posses technical knowledge but at the same time they generate more creative ideas while lead users are those that posses knowledge of underlying technology but their ideas more simple and less original which bring them more easily to realization than with the ideas of ordinary users (Magnusson, 2009, p. 581). Reasons of user's motivation to facilitate user innovation can, of course, differ and depend on characteristics of industry, users, and products and services. In most cases users innovate to improve their lives. On the one hand, they take incentives in innovation because they think of the values and benefits they supposed to get from the innovative product but from the other hand users are aware of their needs but short of technology and costs. Users participate in user innovation because they expect to obtain short-term benefit from their innovations and not always monetary and these benefits can be considered as drivers of creativity, however, companies cannot rely completely on users participation but they should take their ideas as an inspiration for further innovation (Magnusson, 2009, p.582). So, the benefit that companies can take by attracting users is to stay innovative in the long run. Moreover, this leads to value co-creation and deep understanding of customer needs that is very important in customization era.

Covered issues of service innovation concept, its drivers and tendencies have found some links and touched some of the postulates and theories of TQM, sustainable development and indirectly CSR which will be contextualize in the following chapter.

3.8. Brand Management a Stakeholder perspective

3.8.1. Branding as a medium of stakeholders dialogue

Brand is an abstract notion that finds association in human minds with some products and services. We can also characterize brand as an image or reputation related to definite goods/services. Ind (2005) defined that brand itself is something immaterial and represent a transforming idea that turns physical goods and services into something of value that at the same time generates a problem of measuring the value of brand (p.3). But nowadays brand is not only a narrow concept but it includes a lot of aspects and is integrated in organizational approaches, philosophies and strategies. The value of a brand is something that is nowadays even reported in a numerical format on official level by way of announcing and publishing rates. Basically value of a brand is treated as worth of the brand, including financial assets both tangible and "goodwill" (Lynn, 1995). All this brand information undoubtedly reaches company's stakeholders directly or indirectly. Thus, brand delivery cover huge network of interested parties and therefore brand identity and brand massage play important role.

Below given figure by Hatch and Schultz (2009) represents communication model on the way of brand formation. This model consists of internal and external/corporate communication. Besides, Hatch and Schultz (2009) pointed out that employer branding is quite hot issue in HR circles nowadays and if it is done separately from corporate branding programs they can result in the fragmentation of the brand.

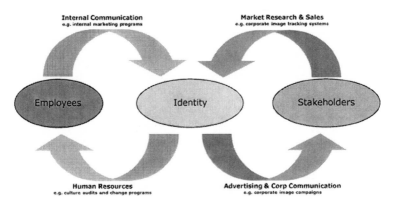

Figure 5: Communication Model   **Source: (Hatch & Schultz , 2009, p126)**

Being an immaterial subject it is difficult to raise a trustful brand. Time and experience is needed to build a trustworthy brand. Brands assume to give expectations and bear information that make customers and other stakeholders critical about them and this can happen from both positive and/or negative sides. However, stakeholders' critics can help the company strengthen its brand, find and correct mistakes, finally revive the brand. Therefore, any feedback is valuable. Moreover, as Hatch and Schultz (2009) noted "the images stakeholders from and communicate among themselves are mirrored back to the organization, providing important feedback that can help a firm to know itself" (p.118). So, brands live long life and over the whole period they can also be changed or reshaped under different conditions that can take place in economics, in organizational management, in social sphere and so on. Ind (2005) gave nice clarification of how brand is integrated in a system stating that "brands drive relationships, relationships liberate knowledge, knowledge generates insight, insight drives innovation, innovation drives transaction, transaction create value, which reframes the brand and so on, and so on" (p.71).

3.8.2. Brand Co-creation

In the previous chapter we gave overview of co-creation with the customers. We have also emphasized that it is important to create value with the customers attracting them to participate thus driving innovation process. But having studied some researches done on the topic of branding we came across an interesting article about branding co-creation. It advocates that not only customers are engaged in the process of co-creation but all stakeholders participate in the formation of brand and creation value.

The authors Hatch & Schultz (2010) considered the concept of co-creation as a continuation of the idea that took place in researches about user-driven product innovation and emphasized that in case of branding co-creation expands to embrace other stakeholders than consumers (p.591). Thus, much attention is given to the consideration of brand meaning and value at the perspective of stakeholders engagement. Particularly, the overview is given through the prism of four "building blocks" - dialogue, access, risk assessment and transparency. Being involved in dialogue stakeholders get a certain access to company information, specific data, organizational culture, etc. Once stakeholders gain access the organization become visible to them and other in their broad network thus disclosing company's managerial practices, decision-making and other related business processes (Hatch & Shultz, 2010, p. 595). The dialogue and access can create brand trust among the stakeholders and this facilitates stakeholders to further participation in brand's life. This makes stakeholders to find the ways to co-create with the company from which side they find feedback and understanding. However, authors discussed that excessive access put some companies' secrets to a risk of being revealed. This immerse transparency is somewhat that lead to the real risk that company takes involving all stakeholders and interests of all parts of organization that is conceptually described by Hatch and Schultz (2010)   as "enterprise brand" which give stakeholders control of brand meaning and ultimately the value it brings to the organization (p.603).

Customers and other stakeholders are the participants of making/creating a brand and this make the relationships between those communities even closer. The output of relationships can contribute to brand sustainability, innovation and continuous improvements.

3.8.3. Behind the brand

Taking a closer look to the brand essence it is important to mention how brand is linked to Corporate Social Responsibility as brand is one that associated with image and reputation.

When defining the concept of CSR we were discussing values of the company and stakeholders that are important for success and for the company to be sustainable. In this regards, while "living the brand" the following three core elements as vision, culture and image – must be aligned in a successful values-based branding strategy (Enquist & Edvardsson, 2009).

Beyond the rise of CSR concern is a "growing evidence to suggest that consumer demand for sustainable goods and services is on the increase" (Collings 2003, p. 159) In the recent years, customers attitude towards ethical friendly and ecologically clean goods has changed. They don't add value to product and service they are introduced or given, they evaluate not only monetary aspect but some other parameters as well and CSR initiative of a company is one of them. Still Collings (2003) mentioned about the research where people said they would prefer environmentally and socially responsible products to those that are not, however, if two products were equal on price and quality, a company's policy on social and environmental issues would be not be deciding for many people. .

Also, image is a core concern and actually introduces brand itself. When linked with CSR initiatives it may have much more favorable and positive effect. But it is still measured within the time span. For example IKEA trademark, reputation and the brand image is the result of 50 years of work contributed by IKEA-co-workers at all levels and all over the world (Enquist & Edvardsson, 2009).

Summarizing, we can say that it is important to build corporate culture and reputation and subsequently brand in customers and stakeholders' eyes based upon company's genuine attempts to improve out life, to solve environmental problems, to help starving and poor children, and to bear continuous concern about our future. Brand is not about products in most cases. Customers' perception of the brand has become more demanding and wider. CSR can serve as an instrument to help customers to see "behind the brand" in essence. But if it really works or not is still being under discussion in academic literature.

3.8.4. Brand and quality

Quality and brand are tightly linked and sometimes are treated as the whole inseparable thing. Quality can serve as an attribute to a brand that facilitates its power, familiarity and popularity. Thinking about brand one understands quality that lies behind certain brand and consequently product under this brand. As we discussed earlier Quality aspects take central place nowadays that is why companies try to integrate quality improvements in all spheres and as such contributing to brand management. All efforts that are done with the quality management system find its reflection in building a strong brand. Customers and stakeholders that are also co-creators of brand are active participants of the process. Brand serves as image and reputation that are based on values that companies conceptualize through their code of conduct, vision and mission. Once direction is defined the brand will definitely be affected. And if the company takes quality as a central objective it should automatically come in mind about the brand.

It should be also mentioned that for services the brand perception can embrace a harder process. As Lynn noted "for brands of intangibles, the problem can be considerably more complex and virtually all of the attributes attached to a service brand are really perceptions created by the service itself and the people and things that provide that service – in other words, the service experience (Lynn, 1995, p.65). And these experiences happen through company-customer or company-stakeholder relationships.

Hatch & Schultz (2009) also emphasized that "services are always tricky to brand because they depend so heavily on the behavior of the employees who deliver them and if it is one thing to brand products, whose quality is predictable, it is quite another to invest in brands for which human variability is significant factor" (p.117)

3.9. Overview of ISO standards, OHSAS 18001, GRI and Global compact

In this chapter we will review some of the international quality standards and reporting guidelines in relation to our research, to examine if there is any link between the quality concepts that we have discussed above and how much does it relate to the theories when it comes to the question of implementation.

ISO 9001 and ISO 14001

International Standard Organization (ISO) is the organization that develops international voluntary standards. ISO aims for fair business globally and protect the different stake holder group (i.e. user and consumer). Further, ISO covers all three dimensions of sustainable development, these are: economic, environment and social (ISO 9000, 2009). The growing need of common standards globally enhanced the development of ISO standards. The reason behind this is the business organizations are expanding their operations and selling their services worldwide. Among ISO standards ISO 9000 series deals with the Quality management system (QMS) of a company. The standard defines QMS as "a management system to direct and control an organization with regard to quality. So far four standards have been introduce in 9000 series. These are ISO 9000:2005, 9001:2008, 9004:2009 and ISO 9011:2002.

Among these standards ISO 9001 deals with the fundamental of QMS. The basic elements of QMS viewed in the following process model. These are leadership, customer focus, process view and continuous improvement (Bergman & Klefsjö, 2010; ISO 9000, 2009)(see figure 6.). This is very much similar to the core values of TQM that we discussed earlier.

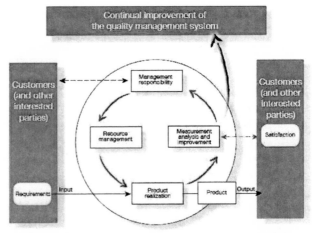

Figure 6: Model of process approach (source: ISO 9000, 2009)

The 7 steps of implementation and maintenance of QMS consists of several criteria:

- First of all it has to engage the top management totally.
- Then it has to identify the process and interactions that are required for QMS. Find and use appropriate technique to implement and maintain the process. This can be done developing ISO 9001 based QMS.
- Further the workforce has to be trained and to implement the system.
- Manage the QMS by measuring, monitoring and analyzing the process through continuous improvement. Third party audit can be done to maintain the process.

Above criteria can easily be linked with the three components suggested by Hellsten & Klefsjö (2000) and the TQM philosophy that has been discussed earlier. Since, the criteria are similar to the components of TQM, for instance identify the core values, and realize the core values using appropriate techniques and use of suitable tools to implement the care values. Further, it has to start with top management's full involvement. This is the foundation of TQM cornerstones.

After implementing ISO 9001 the organization can move to ISO 9004 to upgrade the standard. ISO 9001 and ISO 9004 are compatible.

On the other hand ISO 14001 standards is a widely accepted Environmental Management System (EMS) introduced by International Standards Organization (ISO). Sebhatu and Enquist (2007) suggest EMS that like 14001 can encourage companies and stakeholders thinking towards adopting a TBL thinking. Since, ISO focuses to fulfill the stakeholders' need (ISO 14001, 2009). ISO 14001 EMS offers a standard against which an organization's environmental activities can be assessed. Further, the study states that ISO 14001 certification can be used as driver for sustainable development and value creation (Sebhatu and Enquist 2007). Many researchers have proposed an integration of ISO 9001 and ISO 14001 as they are compatible. That can be possible by adopting ISO 26000 which supports the principles of UN Global compact and is built on the standards of social responsibility (Bergman & Klefsjö, 2010). However, the ISO 14001 is criticized for lack of public reporting.

Global Reporting Initiative

The Global Reporting (GRI) was introduced in 1997 by US non-governmental organization and "Coalition for environmentally responsible economies" and the United Nation environmental program. In the sustainability reporting guidelines GRI is stated as "a long-term, multi-stakeholder, international process whose mission is to develop and disseminate globally applicable Sustainability" (GRI, 2002). Further, GRI has adopted a so called triple bottom line philosophy in order to uphold transparency in writing annual reports (White, 1999). The guideline can be voluntarily adopted by any organization for preparing report on economic, environmental and social issues for representing their activities product or services (GRI, 2002). Furthermore, GRI provides a better reporting structure for companies where stakeholders and environmental issues are taken into account which is not possible by an internally generated report. For the reason, issues like human rights, labor rights and animal requires qualitative assessment rather than quantitative assessment (Waddock et al, 2004). These are issues about which the stakeholders remain concerned of. However, Isaksson and Steimle (2009) argue that GRI reporting guideline is not sufficient for sustainable reporting, since it doesn't fulfill the needs of the customer sufficiently, whereas customer is center of TQM philosophy; whereas Waddock et al (2004) refers it as inconsistent reporting style. This might be ensured through further improvement of the guidelines.

UN Global Compact

On the other hand Global compact can be seen as a voluntary corporate citizenship that was an initiative taken by the United Nations and introduced in 2000 (Enquist et al, 2006). UN Global Compact Upholds four principles on four different areas. These are Human rights labor standards, the environment and anti-corruption (see table 5, next page) The idea of UN global compact is to support and adopt the following principles as core values and implement them in the organizational culture from a global perspective with a stakeholder's view, as Ban Ki-moon the Secretary-General of the United Nations has stated that, "We need business to give practical meaning and reach to the values and principles that connect cultures and people everywhere." (UN Global Compact, 2011, p.4. However, Arevalo and Fallon (2008) argue that the Global Compact evaluation criteria is seriously lacking. Therefore, the success of Global Compact and its contribution to CSR largely depends on how the organizations are using it.

OHSAS 18001

OHSAS 18001 is a voluntary international standard of "occupation health and safety assessment" used as a health and safety management system. It facilitates the organization to maintain occupational health and safety risk. It was developed in response to the high demand of a better work environment. Further, it was designed to be used for certification purpose. However, it is not mandatory to get registered for the certification. The standard can be adopted in voluntarily and the company can declare if it complies with OHSAS standard. Further the standard is ISO 9001 and 14001 compatible means it can easily be adopted and integrated with the above mentioned ISO standards (OHSAS, 2010).

Table 5: Ten Principles of UN Global Compact

	HUMAN RIGHTS
Principle 1	Business should support and respect the protection of internationally proclaimed human rights; and
Principle 2	make sure that they are not complicit in human rights abuses
	LABOR
Principle 3	Business should uphold the freedom of association and the effective recognition of the right to collective bargaining
Principle 4	the elimination of all forms of forced and compulsory labor;
Principle 5	The effective abolition of child labor; and
Principle 6	The elimination of discrimination in respect of employment and occupation
	ENVIRONMENT
Principle 7	Business should support a precautionary approach to environmental challenges;
Principle 8	Undertake initiatives to promote greater environmental responsibility; and
Principle 9	Encourage the development and diffusion of environmentally friendly technologies
	ANTICORRUPTION
Principle 10	Business should work against corruption in all its forms, including extortion and bribery

(Source: UN Global Compact, 2011)

4. Empirical study and analysis

In this chapter we will analyze the case of LEGO. This part will include several chapters and will also follow the conceptual frame that has been developed in the previous chapter.

4.1. Company Profile

LEGO...the story began back in 1934, when the carpenter Ole Krik Kristiansen founded the company with the name LEGO which in translation from Danish words "leg" and "godt" means play good. "Play good" started from wooden toys switching with the advent of plastic to the famous classical bricks. LEGO is family-owned company which has been further ruled by a grandson of Ole Kristiansen Kjeld Kirk Kristiansen for 25 years until he stepped in October 2004 for Jorgen Vig Knudstorp, who is the current Company President and CEO (LEGO, 2010c)..

In 1947 Lego factory bought the first in Denmark plastic injection-moulding machine for production of toys having changed production from wooden material into plastic. This change was also effected by a fire that destroyed a warehouse in 1960 (Mortimer, 2003). In 28 January 2008 the LEGO brick celebrated its 50th anniversary because that day Gotfred Kirk Christiansen filed his patent application with the Danish patent authorities in 1958 (LEGO, 2007b). In 2003 more than 20 billion Lego bricks were produced a year and a Lego set was sold every seven seconds (Mortimer, 2003). In 2010 it amounted to about 3,900 different elements in the LEGO range – plus 58 different LEGO colours and each element may be sold in a wide variety of different colours and decorations, bringing the total number of active combinations to more than 7,500 (LEGO 2010c). Lego brick is not just a toy, its value is added for its educational significance for the kids. Moritimer (2003) stated that LEGO serves consumer education also through its presence in school throughout the world. The many possible ways of combining LEGO components encouraged children to use their imagination and explore their own creative universe (LEGO 2010c).

Nowadays LEGO bricks are sold in more than 130 countries (LEGO 2010c). LEGO has approximately 9000 employees worldwide. Production capacities located to serve in a best way the nearest big markets Europe and USA. The products are manufactured at LEGO Groups' own factories in Denmark, Hungary, Czech Republic and Mexico. In 1968 the company opened its first LEGOLAND in Billund, Denmark, theme park made of millions of bricks (LEGO 2010c) and by so doing the company found opportunity directly to reach the customers. Moreover, the company got closer to the customer through shops, web sites, films, call centers and LEGOLAND parks that later were opened as well in Germany, USA and UK.

It has been many years since the classical LEGO brick was introduced and gained worldwide recognition and in spite of an era of new digital and electronic game, LEGO toy made of bricks remains in demand and at the start of the new millennium was claimed "Toy of the century" (LEGO 2010c). Brand of LEGO is featured by the spirit "only the best is good enough". This slogan makes it clear to understand what company is striving for. True to its motto the LEGO Group has emphasized the importance of high quality throughout its more than 75-year history, ensuring that consumers return to LEGO products again and again (LEGO 2010c).

The companies 1999 to 2004 the company was suffering from losses. Despite its extraordinary hold on the imagination of children around the whole world, the Billund, Denmark, company was in trouble and the Lego Group had lost money four out of the seven years from 1998 through 2004, stating sales drop 30 percent in 2003 and 10 percent more in 2004, when profit margins stood at −30 (Oliver et al., 2007). Lego Group executives estimated that the company was destroying €250,000 ($337,000) in value every day (Oliver et al., 2007).

Major change on the way to recovery was to appoint Jorgen Vig Knudstorp. That time 34, a onetime management consultant who had joined the company in 2001 as a director of strategic development, Knudstorp spent his first weeks as CEO working closely with Kristiansen and the other members of the board and the leadership team to pinpoint the source of the company's problems (Oliver et al., 2007). Action plan was elaborated and implemented in all major areas of company operation that lead to company gradual revitalization. Much of this can be owed to Knudstorp's initial background. He had completed his PhD in business economics, focusing on superior value creation based on the particular configuration of a company's key assets (Face to Face, 2006). During our research paper analysis we will revert to the company's failure and success stories to show the processes and major changes that effected company and LEGO brand on the different stages of its development.

4.2. Revitalization Strategy of LEGO Group.

Here step by step we will analyze how the Quality Management system of LEGO evolved over the time in relation to our research question.

We feel the necessity to analyze the LEGO case elaborately after 2003, since after this period LEGO made the major changes in its organizational structure. However, data before 2003 has also been used for the analysis.

After the consecutive loss of 935 million DKK in 2003 and 1931 million DKK in 2004, LEGO group was almost in the stage of bankruptcy. In this condition in 2004

47

LEGO decided to change the principles of doing business. In the action plan of 2004 under supervision of the new CEO, LEGO decided to make three major changes that consists of the following themes (LEGO, 2004). These are:

- Fundamental change in the way of doing business.
- Re-establish competitiveness by emphasizing on the customers
- Reduce the level of risk by resizing the assets portfolio.

As a part of the action plan LEGO decided to reduce its production cost and operating cost by 20 % through outsourcing 80% of its manufacturing plants to low cost countries such as Mexico, China and Eastern European countries. (LEGO, 2004a; LEGOb, 2006a). Under this policy the Packaging and distribution plant in Enfield was shut down as a result 300 employees lost their job. In the same way 900 employees lost their job in the Billund, Denmark factory. Further LEGO decided to sell its LEGO LAND Parks to improve liquidity of its assets and create a strong financial base for the company (LEGO, 2004a). Finally, under the new policy LEGO decided to establish direct dialogue between LEGO group and LEGO customer, since the company believes that the consumer drives innovation (LEGO, 2005a).

The action plan worked out for LEGO, since the company made a profit of 214 million DKK in 2006 and 1290 million DKK in 2007 (LEGO, 2007a). LEGO portrays this turn back in the business in three stages. The first stage was to stabilize the company and gain control in order to survive. In the second stage LEGO's policy was to develop defensible core of products and to rebalance the capital structure to transform its business. The third stage was to improve core business and prepare for organic growth through brand revitalization (LEGO, 2004a). We will discuss more about the brand revitalization in the following chapter on LEGO Brand Management.

In 2007, the top management decided to integrate sustainability as a new strategy. Under this strategy the second and third stage were declared as a platform of sustainable growth (Figure 7).

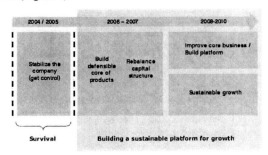

Figure 7 : Building Platform for Sustainable Growth (LEGO, 2007a, p 11)

48

Further, LEGO found stakeholder plays a crucial role for the company in its sustainable growth. As mentioned in the progress report of (2007b)

"Only through dialogue with the stakeholders is it possible to disclose their expectations to the company – and only through meeting these expectations is it possible to ensure long-term, sustainable business".p9.

Within this view LEGO divided its stakeholder's consumers, customer, employees, business partners and suppliers, shareholder and society. Further the expectations of the stakeholder were divided into three areas. These are Value Creation, Brand and Responsibility (LEGO, 2007b). The company states that all stakeholders expect *value creation*. However, this expectation varies among different stakeholder groups. For example customer expects more value in exchange of their money and retailers expects more earning. Moreover, since LEGO is a well known *brand* and the motto of the company is "only the good is best enough" that's why the customer expects better quality and the retailer expects more sales in their stores. Finally, the stakeholder expects that the company will be highly *responsible* in relation to CSR practice base on its brand values. Here, by CSR the company refers to safe and high quality toys, practice of high ethical standards, ensure the security of employee safety etc. (LEGO, 2007b). The above discussed measures undertaken by LEGO can be integrated in following diagram. Here we see that the three areas value creation, responsibility and brand are interdependent.

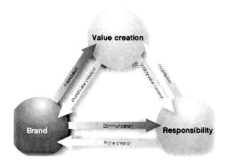

Figure 8: Business Sustainability Model (LEGO, 2007b, p10)

49

4.3. Quality Management System (QMS) in LEGO based on standards

After the recovery stage LEGO started to focus on its quality management system. The company used the motto "only the best is good enough" as a core value in the development of the system and was committed to improve continuously. Therefore, LEGO made an effort to integrate ISO 9001, ISO 14001, ISO 8124 and OHSAS 18001 in its quality management system (QMS). The QMS aims to improve in the area of environmental management, employee health and safety, quality of product and production process (Christensen, 2010). Further LEGO found that it was easy to communicate with its stakeholders using different standards. The former chair of ISO/TC 181, Peter Trillingsgaard explains it in the following way.

> *" Being a global company with manufacturing in several countries and sales in more than 100 countries, the LEGO Group finds International Standards very important. They do not only make our processes and products better but the standards are also a 'language' that authorities, customers and employees understand and value."*
> *(Christensen, 2010, p47).*

In the annual conference of Quality Management and Organizational Development (QMOD) in 2009 the Senior Director of Global Quality Cornelis Versluis declared that LEGO has developed and implemented its Global Quality Management System (QMS) in record time of nine months. In 2008 after re-establishing the financial base, LEGO bought back its three manufacturing plants with diversified group of suppliers and numerous QMS standards. At the same time, the company was also under pressure because of the US legislation on the safety of toy. Further, the company had to certify three of it's cites under ISO 9000:2008 standard. In this situation LEGO developed its Global QMS and within nine weeks certified the first manufacturing plant in accordance to the new QMS (Versluis, 2009a). Here we need to mention that since 1991, ISO 9001 has been used as a principle framework by LEGO to outline its global quality management system. The communication manager Jan Christensen (2010) at the LEGO Corporate Communications department in Billund, Denmark mentions that ISO 9001 was an effective way to introduce the QMS in the new manufacturing sites. Since, most of the quality management personnel are aware of the ISO 9001 requirements so the company could focus more on the internal requirements.

Further, LEGO integrated ISO 14001 and OHSAS 18001 to provide improvements in the areas of environmental, health and safety (EHS) management. LEGO has certified all of its sites in accordance with the above mentioned standards. LEGO group used ISO 14001 as a management tool to improve both physiological and physical work environment, prevent absenteeism, increase employee job satisfaction, reduce the consumption of energy and manage waste. The standards are also used as a tool to implement its core values and to protect the brand both internally and externally (Christensen, 2010). For example, internally LEGO uses the requirements of ISO 14001 to keep its workforce updated regarding the company's policies through its EHS website. And externally ISO 14001 is used in the annual report and sustainability report as a medium to deliver the EHS performance of the company to its stakeholders. Since, in the recent times the stakeholders are more concerned regarding the environmental, health and safety performance of the organizations.

Further, ISO 8124 is used internally to communicate with relevant departments to ensure the product safety of the toys. LEGO has translated the requirements of the standard in a 'product safety handbook'. Finally, LEGO has certified 84% of its sites in accordance with OHSAS 18001 standard to ensure the health and safety of the employees (LEGO, 2010b).

4.4. Communication with stakeholder in relation to LEGO QMS

Quality management is often seen as an uninteresting subject to the employees due to its complexity. To deal with this challenge LEGO developed a simple way to deliver the core values of its global quality management system to its employees. The CEO of LEGO group Jørgen Vig Knudstorp explained it to the Danish magazine Berlingske Nyhedsmagasin in 24 February 2006 in the following way:

> *"We are getting back to something, which we were good at 30-40 years ago: Strong business acumen. In internal communication, I call it "a down-to-earth culture" which is meant positively. Let us not make things too complicated, let us not be too academic, let us just be good businessmen".(Valcon, 2006, p6).*

In order to communicate with the employees the LEGO Senior Director of Global Quality Cornelis Versluis developed a method, where he highlights the three major points of LEGO QMS. 1) The adoption of LEGO QMS drives performance. 2) The adoption process of QMS is a challenge and 3) QMS can easily be adopted through playful learning. (Versluis, 2010). The playful learning was conducted in two steps (Versluis, 2009a).

1. Focused message: In the first step LEGO wanted to deliver the message only in one slide. The slide represented that the QMS in LEGO consists of only five components (figure 9). In the figure we see LEGO has included different kind of stakeholders starting from the supplier to its customers in the process. The foundations of this model are the quality and product safety policies (Versluis, 2009b).

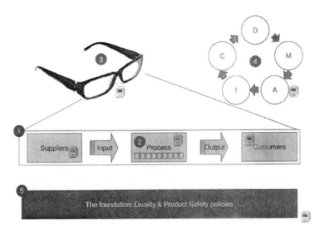

Figure 9: LEGO QMS in one page (Versluis, 2009b, p14)

2. Educational Games: In the second step LEGO designed educational games since its fun to learn from games. The idea is that people will experience the game and make a reflection of the game in their real life (Versluis, 2009a). This process was quite effective since it is fun to learn from experience rather than just reading books.

4.5. Sustainable performance measure of LEGO

Under this chapter we have used the SPM framework to measure the sustainable performance of the company and also to test the link QM with brand management, innovation and CSR practices in LEGO. There will be some repetition of the facts presented earlier in this measurement process. The performance will be measured both internally and externally.

Economic measures

LEGO had revenue of DKK 16,014 million that is 37% higher than the revenue of 2009 that was DKK 11661 million. Profit in 2010 before tax increased to DKK 4,889 million comparison to DKK 2,887 million in 2009. Net profit of 2010 increased to DKK million 3718 comparison to DKK million 2,204 in 2009. (LEGO, 2010a). Overall the company has achieved a 105% growth in the revenue since 2006 (LEGO 2010b.).

The global market share of LEGO increased by 5.9% in comparison with 4.8% of 2009. Currently LEGO is the fourth largest toy manufacturer in the world (LEGO, 2011a). LEGO experienced growth in the market of USA, UK, Russia and Eastern Europe. Therefore, the recent economic performance of LEGO is considerably good.

Table 6: Financial results of LEGO

	2003	2004	2005	2006	2007	2008	2009	2010
Revenue	7196	6704	7027	7798	8027	9526	11661	16014
Profit & Loss	-935	-1931	214	1290	1028	1352	2204	3718

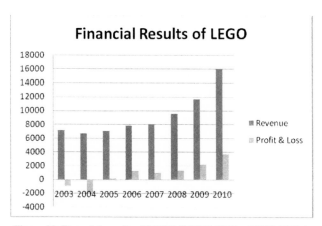

Figure 10: Financial results of LEGO (LEGO, 2007a; LEGO 2009a)

Social Measures

Customer

In accordance to the motto "only the best good enough" LEGO is committed to deliver high quality and safe toys for the children. In this view the company has adopted ISO 8124 developed by ISO/TC 181 and considers it as one of the most important standard for the company (Christensen, 2010). Further, LEGO is working in collaboration with three other toy manufacturers in ISO/TC 181 and the technical committee to improve the standards for toy safety. As a result LEGO received only two product recalls in last seven years that is quite low. Besides, the physical safety of the toys LEGO concerns digital safety of their product. Therefore, LEGO has developed a set of measures to ensure the online safety of its toy named "LEGO Universe Safety Guidelines" in combination with technology, people, community and parental involvement.(LEGO, 2010b)

Employee:

After 2006 so far LEGO has recruited 4,900 new employees (approximate). Currently, the company is employing 8,365 full time employees (figure 11) (LEGO, 2010a)

53

maintaining a good balance in terms of gender diversity. The workforce consists of 4790 female and 5053 male employees this include the part-time employees as well.

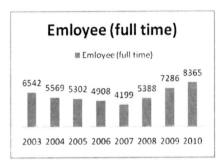

Figure 11: Number of fulltime Employee in LEGO (LEGO, 2007a; LEGO 2009a)

Since the company is expanding rapidly globally, it has become a challenge for the company to communicate with the employees globally and share the company's core values. LEGO finds its brand promises and ISO 14001 as a strong medium to communicate with its employees. Moreover, the company communicates with its employees via its EHS website to keep them update regarding the environmental, health and safety policies of the company (Christensen, 2010). The Company has a policy to adapt the LEGO culture with the Local culture. Further, LEGO has trained 98% of its directors in the area of business integrity and anti-corruption that is a principle of UN Global compact (LEGO, 2010b). Also the company is sharing its Global QMS through playful learning that we have discussed earlier.

LEGO has also declared a Top 10 on the safety of employees. Also, the injury rate was reduced by 38% in the year 2010 (LEGO, 2010b). For this reason the group has a policy to adopt OHSAS 18001 certification in all of its sites with more than 100 employees (LEGO, 2010a).

Suppliers:

Besides the employees LEGO supports the suppliers to be a part of the trade union. Further the company accepts that a worker should not work more that 60 hour/weeks. Since 2006 company is dedicated to ICTI (International Council of Toy industry) care process that is a program to promote ethical manufacturing of toy through a monitoring program. Further, LEGO has conducted 33 external audits in accordance to Code of Conduct that includes the high risk countries and 33 supplier quality awards internally (LEGO, 2010b).

Other stakeholders:

LEGO believes that paying tax will have a positive impact on the society. By doing so the company will gain stakeholders trust and mutual respect (LEGO, 2010b). In 2010 LEGO disbursed DKK 1,171 million that is higher in comparison to DKK 683 million the previous year. Further, LEGO group has formed "The LEGO Foundation" to deliver its service to the poor and unprivileged children. In this view LEGO has set a target to reach 101 million children by year 2015. Among this 101 million only one million children will get the support of the LEGO foundation rest of the 100 million will get the toys through the convention supply chain(LEGO, 2010b).. Further, under the "Care for children in need" program the company will work in collaboration with United Nations High Commissioner for Refugee (UNHCR) and Danish Ministry of Foreign Affairs, public diplomacy and provide used toys to the refugee children as charity. Already 100,420 kilograms bricks have been sent in countries like Ukraine, Turkey, Afghanistan and Haiti   Finally, LEGO is contributing to education system in countries like South Africa and Brazil through its Care for Education Program (LEGO, 2010b).

Environmental measures

Under the planet promise LEGO realizes that energy and waste are two most important factors that have impact on the environment. Further, the company believes it has a direct and positive impact on the financial performance of LEGO and ultimately reduces expense and saves resources. In this view LEGO has already adopted ISO 14001 as EMS and getting benefit from it that we have discussed earlier.

Energy consumption and waste management

LEGO wants to get independence from fossil energy by 2020. As a part of this policy LEGO decided to reduce the energy consumption. Further, LEGO want to decrease the expense for renewable energy, since they have already found some possible way to reduce energy consumption from the investment made on 2009. As a result LEGO's energy efficiency has increased by 60% than the result of 2007 (LEGO, 2010b). Moreover, the company has a goal of going for 100% renewable energy. In terms of waste management LEGO want to achieve a goal of zero waste by recycling its waste. For instance the plastic waste from the moulding machine is reused as a raw material. In the year 2010 LEGO has recycled 87% of its waste and gained competitive advantage from it (figure 12) (LEGO, 2010b).

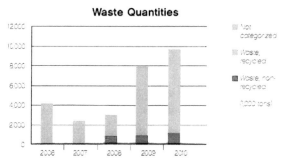

Figure 12: Waste Quantities in LEGO (LEGO,2010b, p5)

TRM-

Integration (different standards): In 2006 LEGO changed its fundamental way of doing business. In this view LEGO has adopted different international standards within the company's global QMS system. Under the global quality management system LEGO integrated several international standards such as ISO certification, EMS, toy safety standard and employee health and safety management standard.

Descriptive/Potential values: After having negative financial results the company wanted to make major changes. The first step was to reduce cost to build a strong financial base. Therefore the company decided to adopt EMS to manage its waste and increase energy efficiency. Further, LEGO identified its stakeholders and divided the stakeholders' expectations in three areas. These were value creation, brand and responsibility and linked it to its QMS. LEGO found brand management as an effective medium to share the company's values with its stakeholders. Also LEGO found customer as a driver of innovation.

Normative/core values: The potential values were brought into practice by adopting the following standards. The standards that LEGO has adopted so far are ISO 9001 for quality management, ISO 14001 for environmental management, ISO 8124 for toy safety and OHSAS 18001 for employee health and safety management. Finally LEGO shared its core values through its four Brand Promises.

Instrumental values/value creation: The above mentioned actions gave LEGO a solid financial growth. Recently the company has been ranked as the fourth toy manufacturer company in the global toy market. The breakdown of the value creation can be found from the following figure.

Figure 13: Value creation in LEGO (LEGO, 2010,p30)

CSR Reporting in LEGO

Till 2005 LEGO was publishing only financial reports. Annual reports are mainly published for the stockholders. However, LEGO has only 4 stockholders from the Kristiansen family, since it is a family business (Kaspersen, 2009). After the shift in the way of doing business LEGO found it important to share its values to its stakeholders as well. In this view from 2006 besides publishing the Annual Reports LEGO started publishing its CSR report. The report was first named as "Sustainability Report" later on the name was changed to Progress Report. The purpose of this report is to share the company's environmental, social and governance (ESG) performance clearly to its stakeholders. The report follows the UN Global Compact principle that was adopted by the company in 2003. LEGO was the first toy making company to join UN Global Compact. Further the report follows guide lines of sustainability reporting from Global Reporting Initiative (GRI). The goal of the report is to create a platform for dialogue with stakeholders like present and future employees, customer, consumer, NGO and local community (LEGO, 2010b). In 2008 LEGO published its third report in form of a magazine that was known as "The Brick". In this report LEGO integrated its four brand promises (Kaspersen, 2009). Since, it was published in form of magazine with stories and articles related to LEGO culture that attracted more readers. In the CSR reporting and communications summit was held in London 2009, Helle Sofie Kaspersen the Vice President Corporate Governance and Sustainability department of LEGO presented this redefined reporting concept. According to Kaspersen the three diversified reporting styles attracted more stakeholders to read LEGO reports, since they could choose the best alternative according to their choice.

After analyzing the companies sustainable performance using the SMP framework we can see that all the indicators are showing positive results. Hence, we can say LEGO is gearing towards sustainability both internally and externally.

4.6. Service innovation in LEGO

As we can see from the company profile the life story of LEGO is exciting. The company is unique and full of ideas, challenges and future perspectives and this is except for what has been already done and achieved. The company name derives from the Danish word *Leg godt*, meaning "play well" and the drive to innovate was deeply embedded in the corporate culture (Oliver et al., 2007) We are going to concentrate on the innovative power that LEGO embraces and we are going to reveal the sources of LEGO inspiration and analyze tools and strategies that help LEGO to stay innovative.

When it comes to LEGO we found out 2 types of innovations that are carried on. The first is technological innovation that is implementation of new up-to-date technology, equipment, material in the production that are directed on reducing of environmental impact through company's production. And the second type is product/service innovation that basically is embedded in LEGO bricks and concepts. These 2 types of innovation have equal importance for the company and continue innovation of both aimed towards sustainable development.

Coming to the recent years this type of technical innovation is integrated in LEGO approach "Design4Planet" (D4P) aiming to achieve sustainable product design (LEGO, 2010b). It states that production of LEGO toys requires substantial consumption of raw materials, energy, and packaging. Moreover, utilization of products made from polymers is a long-term process. All mentioned made company to think of the scarcity of resources and environmental issues. To this, company strives for transparency with stakeholders in communicating about composition of product and tries to collaborate with suppliers in a way to share strategical approach towards mutual solutions undertaken against unfriendly production (LEGO, 2010b). The approach that lies in innovation is based on improving production leading to reducing of environmental damage which in its turn leads to sustainable development. The company is trying to elaborate and implement this concept in 5 directions: material chemistry, environmental certification (ISO standards, UN Global compact), reduced and compostable print and packaging, design for disassembly, return solutions. Design for disassembly is a target towards zero waste and is important in making base element materials being reused. And in this way innovation is very crucial for LEGO in its operations. Thus, LEGO is trying to innovate coveringthe whole product life cycle starting from distractin of raw material till the products' next life and evaluate its probable unfavorable effects during the production stages (LEGO, 2010b, p. 10).

Figure 14: Closed loop value chain in LEGO (LEGO 2010b, p10)

In the theoretical overview we pointed out about the shift from Goods-Dominant Logic to Service-Dominant Logic. This evidently can be exemplified on LEGO as well. Earlier in its development the company was focusing on production making toys first from wood and then from plastic bricks and so satisfying customers in primary need to play. But the overall market development and ongoing processes of servicization and customization as well as increasing competition corrected company strategic plans and generated new ideas. The company's positioning is not only to produce toys to play but to learn by playing. Customer is developing new skills and creativity that can be called as new customer experiences through products. Moreover, in 1968 the company opened its first LEGOLAND, theme park made of millions of bricks (LEGO Company Profile, 2010). In this way the company find opportunity directly to reach the customers. The Company not only sells 20 billion bricks per year but stays in contact with customer through shops, web sites, films, call centers and LEGOLAND parks, where the parks were set up as showcase for the product, and created an opportunity to experience LEGO brand (Kaisen Different, 2011). This step make relationships with the customers more exciting and more crucial for identifying their needs by talking to them, by creating customer experience in the place of attraction that was not possible before. The LEGO customer became visible. The move away from just Goods-Dominant Logic has happened. The value in exchange having existed before turned into value-in-use. LEGO became to cooperate with customers/users enabling them to create value with the company.

Year 2005 was the milestone for the adopting a new strategic step for future implementation. Thus, one of the company focus was setting up "Dialogue between the LEGO Group and LEGO consumers to drive innovation" (LEGO 2005a). This step was very important and management looked forward period 2006-2008 to be based on involving stakeholders in product development and process improvement rather than on sales growth. In 2006 the company took focus on close cooperation and contact with the users. At this perspective the company increased dialogue with loyal users through number of channels including direct sales (LEGO 2006b). Furthermore, the company considers this direct involvement of users important for innovative power. At this perspective LEGO has organized a special body called The Executive Innovation Governance Group that was in charge for the concept with the main idea - "input from customer communities supported by CED (Community, Education and Direct)" and the areas of innovation included customer interaction (communities, customer service), sales channel (retailer, direct to customer) (Sebhatu, 2011).

The new era of co-creation with customers started after the company provided to all users a license to hack. The company decided instead of suing those, who hacked into the software after the launch of successful robotics product, gave them an official access by licensing and this resulted in an overwhelmingly positive response from the brand community (Hatch & Schultz, 2010, p. 596).

It turned out to be important to the LEGO Group to have close contact with its fans and consumers throughout the world and to this end, the Group engages in many initiatives to strengthen ties between LEGO enthusiasts and the Group (LEGO, 2010c).

Fans of LEGO are introduced by different age groups including even adults fan group. There is a LEGO Club with members aging 6-12 years that can show each other's work and find inspiration within the exchange. A special magazine is issued for this members group. The big community of adults fan gathered in the group AFOL (Adults Fans of LEGO) – it's a whole community of adults who are equally mad for the product as kids and parents. The best known and huge network of fans is probably LUGNET, which describes itself as a community of Lego enthusiasts (Brandchannel, 2011). This biggest of the user-online brand communities was founded in 1988 by American AFOLs Todd Lehman and Suzanne Rich Gree and today LUGNET represents growth and boasts of international membership aiming at exchange of LEGO brick construction concepts (Hatch & Schultz, 2010, p. 597).

Internet has given great possibility for the groups to be united and to share their creativeness. Special softwares are installed that present both educational and innovative value. Lego offers Internet interactivity opportunities that directly involve the user in construction, and offer direction and feedback throughout the process (Brandchannel, 2011) .For example, LEGO Design byMe is one of the tools that help users to make their own virtual models by using the professional special application LEGO Digital Designer where creators can exhibit their models or find inspiration and new ideas (LEGO , 2010c).

LEGO Top management realized from monitoring websites, getting involved online with fans activities, dialogues and visiting some events organized by AFOLs group that people are very serious about playing LEGO and that they can contribute to the coolness of LEGO brand. This engagement can create value for the company and fan are eager to co-create with the company (Hatch & Schultz, 2010, p. 597). To this, the interview with LEGO CEO Mr. Jorgen Vig Knudstorp proves this fans innovativeness: "We were creative company but no innovation were coming out... These consumer insights grew out of the accident when we find out the fact that our fans were much more innovative with LEGO than we haven't been for while and instead of defining on our own we involved them......" (Knudstorp, 2009).

The Company went further making talented users be designers and giving them access to participate in the product designing functions. Thus, in 2005 LEGO launched an Ambassador Program for users. Every year the company recruit around 50 dedicated users from brand communities all over the world to work short periods in LEGO innovation facilities (Hatch & Schultz, 2010, p. 598). This is unique merge of users and employees working in the same areas in corporate programs and in product innovation generate knowledge and experience exchange. People united by the same work and passion are the source of great contribution. As Hatch & Schultz (2010) stated "this activity contributed to the co-creation of several product innovations" (p.598). Besides, some fans turned out their passion of building and creating to became professionals which were recognized by LEGO Group as business partners and in 2011 LEGO Group had 11 Certified Professionals (LEGO, 2010c).

Except for mentioned above groups, programs there are also such activities that happen several times in a year as Visiting tours (LEGO Inside Tour) that invites the most active fans from all over the world to visit company. During the tour all invited guests can have a look around company, to learn about history, culture and values, to get acquainted more closely with the product, modeling and production process.

Close collaboration with fans, listening to them, providing them with tools and access increased LEGO's innovative power. Users became the main source of innovation for LEGO. In interview LEGO CEO Mr. Jorgen Vig Knudstorp emphasized that "users helped in the process of turning around the company because they told was LEGO was about and the next step was to bring these people into driving innovation in the company" (Kundstorp, 2009)

The analysis shows that company dedicates much of its attention to innovation and this technological and customers innovation types find its reflection in innovation at systematic level involving both technology, stakeholders. LEGO embraces also these types of innovation with its new role of customer as a co-creator and users innovation, described by Magnusson (2009), where the users are involved in the process. "Innovation is also a supply chain issue, and sometimes the supply chain can provide ideas for consumer- or customer-driven innovation" (Oliver et al., 2007). All these create preconditions for company towards continuous improvements and sustainability.

4.7. LEGO Brand Management: A Stakeholder perspective.

Massage from CEO Jorgen Vig Kundstorp in Progress Report 2010 (LEGO, 2010b) stated :

> *The LEGO brand is known and loved worldwide for its ability to offer children a*
> *play experience. With not only the bricks but the LEGO experience itself being*
> *passed on from one generation to the next, the brand is constantly renewed and*
> *sustained, thereby enabling us to fulfill our mission of inspiring and developing*
> *the builders of tomorrow (p. 6)*

The statement gives a short characteristic of strong brand built on such foundations as unique play, experience, history, heritage, renovation that in combination lead to sustainability. Besides, Brand of LEGO is featured by the spirit "only the best is good enough". This slogan makes it clear to understand what company is striving for and What is the goal and possible ways to reach it? Using secondary data we will try to analyze more detailed what stands behind the brand, how company is creating its image and how co-creation with customers and other stakeholders affect LEGO brand.

Every brand, of course being associated with product, has its own history. Some are more successful, others are less. LEGO is a brand that has been known for years from both sides. Having studied literature, official website we realized that LEGO had ups and downs in its development before occupying a stable position and being named one of the world's largest toy manufacturers and the largest in construction toys (LEGO, 2010c). And we will analyze how company now is managing its progress and making efforts towards bringing value to the stakeholders.

The LEGO Company corporate brand was created in 1932 exactly when the company for the production of wooden toys was created by Ole Kirk Christiansen, a carpenter from rural Denmark (Hatch & Schultz , 2003). The Company brand unified whole product range under one brand for a long time but with the appearance of new underlying lifestyle products, software and accessories caused the fragmentation of brand and the Company Top Management decided to change the company corporate strategy while staying with the main LEGO's heritage (Hatch & Schultz , 2003).

Notably, in 2002 LEGO invested many resources in building up the LEGO brand (LEGO 2002a). One of the steps was company's investment in a Brand Retail concept that was directed to get closer contact to the customers. This year was characterized with many attempts of product copying and plagiarism that put company in a competitive position but nevertheless company could hold its place (LEGO 2002a). The next prominent year for LEGO brand after the years of a recession was year 2006 that was called "Revitalization of the group and LEGO Brand" (LEGO 2006a). The strategical goal was to focus on the entire company and its process, procedures, structure and approach to the stakeholders (LEGO 2006a).

The quality has been set up as a core of a brand. This makes LEGO brand promises to be in consistency with the policies and strategies directed towards continuous improvements, value creation and sustainability (Figure 15). The word LEGO itself denotes from Danish "leg" and "godt" as "play well". Official website narrates that the motto "Only the best is good enough" was created by Ole Kirk Kristiansen, founder of the company and inventor of LEGO bricks, and "today we still involve that spirit in every way we operate and this means that we do our best to make a positive impact on areas such as: human rights, working environment, environment, charity etc." (The LEGO Group, 2011)

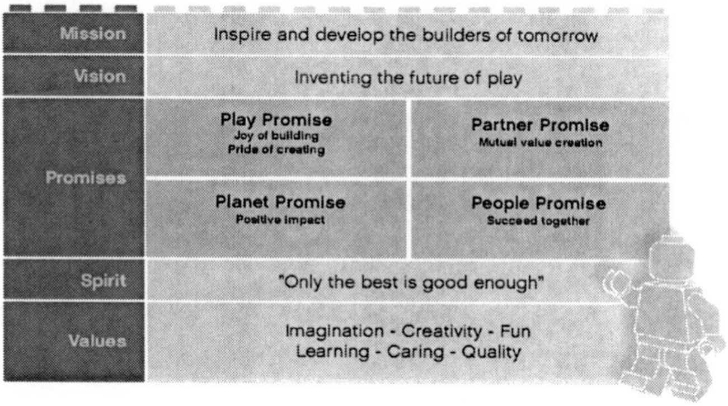

Figure 15 : The brand promises of LEGO (Lego, 2010,p8)

Companies promises encompass commitment towards ensuring a fun and joy by creating and building, towards creating value with stakeholders and succeeding together as a team. Based on the promises the company chose the direction to strengthen the brand together while implementing and realizing the main strategy.

Thus, LEGO outlined future directions which except for expanding market shares and investing in emerging markets include (The LEGO Group, 2011b)

Development of innovative new products In addition to ongoing product development based on the existing core portfolio, the LEGO Group will develop innovative new products which are ideally suited as Lego products, yet never seen before).

Expansion of "direct to consumer" activities . Currently the LEGO Group has already direct contact to consumers using its own sales channels, clubs, collaboration programs, theme parks, etc. But its challenge and aim is to get even closer to consumers through greater contact and by expanding offers available direct to consumers.

Expansion of LEGO Education. This direction is related to learning value that company is going to provide by means of growing in the area of educational materials for preschools, schools and educational institutions all over the world.)

The company promotes its brand values: Creativity, Imagination, Learning, Fun and Quality. These values are incorporated in all company's main function and areas.

The company faced all competition chases that were caused by digital and electronic progress and launched their own product in response (LEGO MINDSTROMS, LEGO Digital Designer, LEGO Interactive, etc) but this again generated problem related to brand management incoherence. There were too many products and names that it was difficult to manage the brand under one umbrella. Moreover, Hatch & Schultz (2003) stated in their article "the Cycles of Corporate Branding" that in LEGO Brand Management "product categories and communication channels are organizationally fragmented and poorly designed" and that company needs to develop a stronger foundation for the LEGO brand (p.9)

However, even with the launch of the digital and electronic games and toys, the LEGO stays on foundation of classical brick, even having been going through different ages and know-how implementation and incorporating a new technology in its products a long the way (LEGO C, 2010).

Talking about the Brand dissemination Hatch & Schultz (2003) pointed out that "fragmented character of a LEGO brand was partly due to organizational processes involved in managing the brand" and they introduced a model called Vision-Culture-Image model that identified organizational challenges of a brand related to vision, culture and image (p.9)

Figure 16: The Vision-Culture-Image (VCI) Model (Hatch & Schultz , 2003)

The model describes brand management with its possible changes in organizational structure from 3 perspectives: Top Management that define vision, employees that absorb corporate culture and live brand's values and stakeholders that precept company image from outside.

LEGO employer branding includes several initiatives. The one called LEGO Brand School was developed to get employees to align themselves behind the LEGO brand (Hatch & Schultz, 2009). Then, the company focused on hiring people, especially in the places where the direct contact with customer occur, who "were genuinely motivated by bringing the best out of others who have the communication, thinking and emotional skills to make it happen" (Kaisen Different, 2004, p. 2). This internal communication proved that branding expanded from the product-consumer relations of product branding to company-stakeholder relations (Hatch & Schultz, 2009).

We noticed that LEGO Brand is linked to CSR and triple bottom line thinking through company's promises. Focusing on "planet promise" LEGO is accounting for environmental issues, on "people promise" and "partner promise" is communicating and delivering massage within communities and stakeholders. Moreover, through "play promise" LEGO Brand drives innovation where the customers are co-creators of a product design and bringing this innovative power they serve as well as LEGO brand co-creators.

After reading secondary data taken from interview, reports and some articles we analyzed that LEGO Brand Management is co-created through such major participants as: customers/users, other stakeholders (supply chain), and employees. We cannot generalize them with the one word stakeholders because they fulfill different function in creating brand (although in theory they are known as stakeholders). All those contributors to brand formation are important and play their own role in LEGO Brand management linking it with the main concepts of TQM and CSR through LEGO promises, values, commitment and stakeholders dialogue.

4.8. A critical evaluation of the analysis

In this chapter the researcher will evaluate quality management system of LEGO critically in relation to the CSR practice, use of service innovation and brand management of LEGO based on the analysis and the theoretical and conceptual frame that has been developed and discussed above.

After examining the case we found that the success of LEGO came in three phases. In the first phase major changes were made in top management when Jorgen Vig Knudstorp was appointed as CEO who is the first person to run the business outside Christiansen family. This created opportunity for LEGO to identify and integrate new values to the company culture apart from the family values. We see it as a major change since the foundation of quality management is top management's commitment. And the first major three changes the top management made were a fundamental change in the way of doing business, building strong relations with its customers and changes in the assets portfolio. In this approach LEGO started with cost cutting policy by firing employees, selling fixed assets and outsourcing its manufacturing plants. This helped LEGO to reduce the expenses and recover from the losses. Therefore, if LEGO falls in losses again in future this might result into downsizing the number of employees globally, since LEGO has already adopted this as a practice in the organizational culture. Selling the fixed assets also helped LEGO to show better profit margin in the annual reports in its survival stage. At the same time considering the customers as the most important stakeholder was an important change in the first stage since customer is the centre of quality management philosophy.

Nevertheless, we also found that the company went through continuous improvement and major changes in its journey. Introduction of business sustainability model in 2007, introducing the brand promises (play, people, partner and palnet) in 2009 and developing the value chain to show the ESG performance in 2010 are examples of continuous change, innovation and improvement. Re-defining the stakeholders' expectations in the company's sustainability model was a major step since it co-created value for the company afterwards. This participation of the secondary stakeholder, besides the primary stakeholders played a major role in the success of LEGO with the progress of time. Different reporting concepts and brand management were successfully used to establish dialogue with stakeholder. We believe the commitment for wider community will help LEGO to build strong brand image globally in future.

Further, the integration of different standards were efficiently used as a common language to share the company's quality measures with its employees, this was a challenge since the company is expanding globally. Moreover, integrating the environmental management and health and safety management within the global QMS facilitated the company to use its resources efficiently. This is a good example of considering the social and environmental bottom line that ultimately leads to economic growth. Therefore, we see CSR as a core value of LEGO quality management in relation to triple bottom line.

Further, LEGO considers communication with the stakeholder as an important part of TQM system. First of all, the three reporting concepts attracted a wide array of stakeholder. Secondly, internal communication with the employees through playful learning was found effective. Finally, EHS website was used to share the company's culture with its employees, so they can remain in one page globally and stays update regarding LEGO's quality policy.

Moreover, we found the company to be very innovative. Its continuous innovation based on finding technological solutions for ecologically friendly production corresponds to the company's focus on sustainability and sustainable development. Besides, the company tries to attract its suppliers and stakeholders towards the same direction - continuous improvement and sustainability. For a long time LEGO has been working on updating its technology, implementing standards, deliberating different programs on minimization of environmental impact through production but there is issue of investments and costs behind that. Modern technology, innovation and quality cannot be compromised if the company wants to go for sustainability. From the analysis we can see that company has huge plans and ideas on development in that direction. From the other hand whether the company is ready and has a backup plan in case of unstable economical situation and other unpredictable force major? Will LEGO be able to remain "afloat" and call for sustainability when one day the company will be forced to cut costs, personnel as this had happened once before? Now LEGO is enjoying its prosperity and stability and the results of hard-working years are visible. The years of recession and then recovery helped LEGO to define the focus and as analysis showed this focus was a right one and now it is important to keep this position.

LEGO is a company which well-known for its permanent innovations implementation. But the fact that LEGO is a manufacturing company, doesn't narrow the integration of services and co-production with customers that have become a part of LEGO thinking and development. Therefore, customer innovation highly integrated in company business and development functions. From the one hand it seems to be fascinating how company engages customers-designers through different clubs, forums, Ambassador Programs but from the other hand will not the customers and users feel to be used one day? The customers contribute a lot of their ideas and experiences and even though now it is based on enthusiasm and company's encouragement will this remain in the future? The company generates profits and this could not affect at least some not to think about it in benefiting way for themselves as well.

There is a very close merge of company and users. We consider the company gives excessive access and as Hatch & Schultz (2010) pointed out "this transparency exposes the company to added risk". And even though we mentioned in theoretical overview that the roles of producer and consumer are not distinct talking about Service-Dominant logic we think that there should be some boundaries. Currently the company is benefiting from this relationships but what will happen in the long-term run? Will it help to sustain? This will remain a question.

Also, investigating LEGO approach to innovation we can figure out sources and drivers that lead to the innovations to be implemented. The driver of innovation for LEGO is also related to the servicisation and customization tendency that we defined and the fact that LEGO is introducing services which are going in hand with the physical product prove the theoretical point. LEGO is cooperating with end users aiming not only at creating loyal relationships but because of seeing users as important and potential source of service innovation. Doesn't this put a claim and buzz on LEGO itself that company can do nothing without its fans and users?

Further, LEGO is one of the few brands which name can be associated with quality, joy and success. Financial performance, brand awareness, CSR-initiatives have strengthen the brand.

We came to the conclusion that LEGO Brand is tightly linked to innovation, CSR and quality. Quality is already value of a brand that lies behind and is represented in company's motto "only the best is good enough". Through brand promises the company committed to contribute to positive impact on environment through production appealing to mutual co-creation and towards success that can be achieved while cooperating closely together with stakeholders. This is the same concept that CSR calls to. Communicating with the stakeholders and delivering them brand messages and brand core values lead to the thinking in the same direction and following the same values. Therefore, brand serves as a medium for stakeholder dialogue. As we said before co-creation with the users/fans/customers result in products innovation and moreover, this lead to brand co-creation with stakeholders.

Analyzing brand development we noticed that LEGO has built its strong brand image very fast and even in recession times LEGO didn't lose it. Internal problems of a company didn't harm the brand. On the contrary we consider that Company got its fame back due to strong brand position. This is a good example how brand can help to revive the company.

We found Vision-Culture-image Model introduced by Hatch & Schultz (2003) to have some of the components that similar to the concepts in CSR and TQM, for example the same pillar as employees, Top management, stakeholders. The company expands its brand delivery through employees on the corporate level while Top Management defines main strategic directions, vision and observe stakeholders perception regarding company's image from outside.

5. Finding and conclusion

To summarize we found LEGO as a very innovative company that went through continuous modification and has been striving for improvement and growth. In this chapter we will present our findings and conclude our research on the LEGO case.

In the case of LEGO we see the company attempts to integrate a wide array of stakeholders within the company's quality management system directly and indirectly. For example, the company has a list of six stakeholder consumers, customer, employees, business partners and suppliers, shareholder and society. However, the company has also considered taxpaying to the state and involving the NGO as responsible act. So we can say the LEGO is slowly moving towards a TRM system from a TQM system. Since, stakeholder are not the centre of the of TQM cornerstones. Here we see CSR as a core value adopted by the company that leads LEGO group towards mutual value creation for itself and its stakeholders.

Further, we found that the company felt the necessity to adopt more than one international quality standard within the LEGO quality management system proves that one quality standard is not enough to fulfill the company and its stakeholder's expectation. Moreover, we found that the integration of quality management and environmental management system were beneficial for the firm. In this way the firm also realized its operant resources for example strive for renewable energy and waste management. Adopting new quality standards such as ISO 26000 can be helpful in this view, since it follows the UN Global Compact principles that share the same dimensions with TBL concept.

We found LEGO was quite innovative in terms of communication with its stakeholder. We believe due to limited number of shareholder LEGO obtain more opportunity to focus toward its stakeholders. The three reporting concepts in LEGO were found effective in terms sharing the company's core values with its stockholders, especially The Brick magazine published by LEGO is a new and effective concept. Over the years LEGO innovated new and effective way to communicate with its stakeholders. Presentation of the core values through different models in the progress report and annual report was simple and easy to understand. Moreover, the report follows internationally accepted guidelines and principle that makes the reports more authentic to the readers. Further, the concept of Playful Learning and communication via EHS website was found quite effective to communicate with employees.

Our study indicates already indicates that LEGO is innovative company striving for sustainability. Thus, innovation is implemented both on the technological level and product/service level. Co-creation with users and customers is another aspect that company pays great attention to. Co-creating with customer, listening to customers' needs, closely communicating with customers generate value co-creation. This approach is driven by the overall processes of servicization and customization that are going on in economy. The concerns are related to the possibility of a company to stay innovative without users and customers that has been driving company's service innovation greatly. The other concern is whether company can stay sustainable without cost compromising on main technological investment in case of unstable economical situation.

Continuous innovation and improvement is one of the components of TQM and one of the approaches of TRM. Besides, the other link that the same as TQM concept calls for is that service innovation is focusing on customer. Covered issues of service innovation concept, its drivers and tendencies have found some links and touched some of the postulates and theories of TQM, sustainable development and indirectly CSR.

The quality has been set up as a core of LEGO brand. This makes LEGO brand promises to be in consistency with the policies and strategies directed towards continuous improvements, value creation and sustainability.

Brand of a LEGO Company has strong power and helped company to overcome difficulties in a certain times of recession. Moreover, company try to create awareness and brand co-creation through stakeholder' dialogue. Thus, communicating closely with customers LEGO spread out brand massages. To this, LEGO employees work as Brand Ambassadors directly approaching customers.

These interrelations prove that behind all considered concepts in this paper, there are some similar components and actors. If we visualize stakeholder as the centre of the TQM then we will realize how closely CSR, Service Innovation and Brand management are linked to the concept of TQM. And in case of LEGO this link definitely gears the company towards sustainable development. Finally, this phenomenon is easier to explain with the help of TRM since it considers stakeholder as the core of doing business.

Reference

Books and Jornals

Averalo J A & Fallon F T (2008) Acessing corporate responsibility as contribution to global governance : The case of the UN Global Compact *Corporate Governance* vol.8 no.42008, pp.456-470

Bergman, B. & Klefsjö, B. (2003). *Quality from Customer Needs to Customer Satisfaction.* 2nd ed. Lund: Studentlitterature.

Bergman, B. & Klefsjö, B. (2010). *Quality from Customer Needs to Customer Satisfaction.* 3rd ed. Lund: Studentlitterature.

Bryman, A. & Bell, E. (2007) *Business research methods.* Oxford University Press, USA.

Bessant, J. & Davies, A. (2007). "Managing Service Innovation".In: DTI (ed). *Innovation in Services.* London: DTI. pp. 61-97

Collings, R. (2003). Behind the Brand: is business socially responsible? *Consumer Policy Review.* Sep/Oct Vol 13, No.5 pp. 159-165

Christensen, J. (2010). LEGO Group seeking perfection Using ISO Standard. *ISO Focus* + Volume 1, No. 3, March 2010, ISSN 1729-8709

Deming, W.E. (1986) *Out of the Crisis.* Massachusetts: Cambridge University Press

Enquist, Bo., Johnson, M. & Skalen, P. (2006). Adoption of corporate social responsibility – incorporating a stakeholder perspective. *Quality Research in Accounting & Management*, Vol 3(3),

Edvardsson, B. & Enquist, B. (2009). *Value-based Service for Sustainable Business: Lessons from IKEA.* Newyork: Routledge.

Elkington, J. (1997). *Cannibals with Forks – The Triple Bottom line of the 21st Century.* Oxford: Capstone publishing

Edvardsson, B. & Enquist, B.M. (2008) *Value-based Service for sustainable business.* Routledge, UK

Enquist, B. & Sebhatu, S.P. (2007), ISO 14001 as a driving force for sustainable development and value creation, *TQM Magazine*, 19, 5, pp. 468-482

Face to Face (2006) *Info: Jorgen Vig Knudstorp.*

Garvin, D.A. (1984), 'What Does "Product Quality" Really Mean?', *Sloan Management Review*, 26, 1, pp. 25-43, Business Source Premier, EBSCO*host*, viewed 16 May 2011.

Grant. R. M., Shami. R. & Krishnan R. (1994). TQM's Challenge to Management Theory and Practice. *Sloan Management Review/Winter 1994, 35(2)*, pp.24-35

GRI (2002), *Sustainable Reporting Guidelines 2002*, Global Reporting Initiative, Amsterdam.

Gill, A. (2008). *Corporate Governance as Social responsibility*: A Research Agenda.

Ghauri, P. & Grönhaug, K. (2005) *Research methods in business studies: A practical guide.* Prentice Hall

Gummesson, E. (2000) *Qualitative methods in management research.* Sage Publications, Inc.

Hossain, A & Neng, B. N. (2010). *The role of Corporate Governance and Corporate Social Responsibility in Business expansion: The Case of Grameen Bank.* Masters Thesis. Karlstad Business School [Unpublished]

Hatch, M. J & Schultz, M. (2003). The Cycles of Corporate Branding: The Case of LEGO Company. *California management Review*, Vol.46, No.1, pp. 6-26

Hatch, M. J & Schultz, M. (2009). Of Bricks and Brands: From Corporate to Enterprise Branding. *Organizational Dynamics*, Vol. 38, No 2, 117-130

Hatch, M. J & Schultz, M. (2010) Toward a theory of brand co-ccreation with implications for Brand Governance. *Brand Management* Vol. 17, 8, 590–604

ISO 9000 (2009) *Selection and use of the ISO 9000 family of standards.* Geneve.

Isaksson R & Steimle U (2009) What does GRI reporting tell us about corporate sustainability. *The TQM Journal* Vol.21No.2,2009 pp.168-181

Ind Nickolas (2005) *Beyond Branding : How the New Values of Transparency and Integrity Are Changing the World of Brand.* London: Kogan Page Ltd

Juran, J. M. (1999), *Jurans Quality Handbook*, 5th ed. Newyork : McGraw-Hill

Kaspersen, H. S. (2009) How to make a report – that will be read. *The Corporate Responsibility Reporting and Communication Summit.* London, November 25-26, 2009.

Klefsjö, B. & Hellsten, U. (2000). TQM as a management system consisting of value technique and tool, *The TQM Magazine*, 12(4), 238-244

Lee, T. W. (1999) *Using Qualitative Methods in Organizational Research* California: SAGE Publications Inc.

Lovelock, C & Wirtz, J (2007). *Services Marketing: people, technology, strategy.* Pearson Prentice Hall.

Lynn B. U. (1995). *Building Brand Identity. A Startegy for Success in a Hostile Marketplace.* New York: John Wiley & Sons, Inc.

Michel, S., Brown, S. W. & Galtan, A.S.(2008). An expanded and strategic view of discontinious innovations:deploying a service-dominant logic. *Journal of the Academy of science* 36: 54-66

Merriam, S. B. (1998). *Qualitative Research and Case Study Applications in Education.* San Francisco: Jossey-Bass Publishers.

Molina-Azorín, J, Tar, J, Claver-Cortés, E, & López-Gamero, M. (2009), 'Quality management, environmental management and firm performance: A review of empirical studies and issues of integration', *International Journal of Management Reviews*, 11, 2, pp. 197-222.

McAdam, R & Lenard, D. (2003) Corporate Social Responsibility in Total Quality Management context. *Corporate Governance*, 3(4), p36-45.

Magnusson P. (2009). Exploring the Contributions of Involving Ordinary Users in Ideation of Technology-based Services. *Product Innovation Management,* 26:578-593

Mortimer, R. (2003). Building Brand out of Bricks. *Brand Strategy*, April/2003, pp.16-19

Newman W. L (1998) *Social Research Methods: Qualitative and quantitative approaches,* 3rd edition, Pearson Education, Inc, USA.

Normann, R. & Ramirez, R. (1993). From Value Chain to Value Constellation: Designing Interactive Strategy. *Harward Business Review* (07-08), pp.65-77

Oliver K., Samakh E. & Heckmann P. (2007). Rebuilding Lego, Brick by Brick. *Strategy+business, issue* 48 Autumn, pp.2-6

Sureshchandar, G., Rajendran, C., & Anantharaman, R. (2002). The relationship between management's perception of total quality service and customer perceptions of service quality. *Total Quality Management, 13*(1), 69-88.

Saunders, Mark, Lewis, Philip & Thornhill, Adrian. (2009) *Research methods for business students.* Upplaga 5. ed. Harlow: Financial Times Prentice Hall.

Sebhatu, P. S. (2008) *"Sustainability Performance Measurement for sustainable organizations: beyond compliance and reporting,"* 11[th]QMOD International Conference, Helsingborg – Sweden , August 2008

Sebhatu, P. S. (2011). Total Quality Management Module, *Service Management & Marketing.* Karlstad University, unpublished

Spohrer and Maglio (2008) Toward Systematic Service Innovations to Accelerate Co-Creation of Value. Production and Operations Management 17 (3), pp. 238-246

Taguchi, G. & Wu, Y. (1979) *Introduction to off-line quality control*

Valcon (2006) *The LEGO Group introduces new radical value chain management framework.* Valcon publication

Voss, C. and Zomerdijk L. (2007). "Innovation in Experiential Services – An Empirical View". In: DTI (ed). *Innovation in Services*. London: DTI. pp. 97-134

Vargo, S. L. & Lusch R. F. (2004). Evolving to a New Dominant Logic for Marketing. *Journal of Marketing*, 68, pp.1-17.

Vargo Stephen L., Maglio Paul P., Akaka Melissa Archpru (2008). On value and value co-creation: A service systems and service logic perspective. *European Management Journal (*26), pp. 145– 152

Versluis, C. A. (2009a) *New QMS in LEGO at record time.* News Future Formula News Letter

Versluis, C. A. (2009b) *Quality by Heart*, 12th QMOD conference, Verona Italy Italy (August 2009), P.14

Versluis, C. A. (2010) *By the book & by heart: The importance of playful learning.* Lecture notes.

Vogel, D.J. (2005) *Is There a Market for Virtue? The Business Case For Corporate Social Responsibility.* California

White, A.L. (1999), "Sustainability and accountable cooperation: Society's rising expectation on business", *Environment*, Vol 41 (8), p30-43

Waddock, S, & Bodwell, C (2004), 'Managing Responsibility: WHAT CAN BE LEARNED FROM THE QUALITY MOVEMENT?', *California Management Review*, 47, 1, pp. 25-37, Business Source Premier, EBSCO*host*, viewed 19 May 2011.

Waddock, S, Bodwell, C, & B. Graves, S (2002), 'Responsibility: The new business imperative', *Academy of Management Executive*, 16, 2, pp. 132-148, Business Source Premier, EBSCO*host*, viewed 19 May 2011

Yin R. K. (2003) *Case Study Research. Design and Methods*, London: Sage

Electronic Journals:

Brandchannel, 2011.[Electronic]. Available
http://www.brandchannel.com/features_profile.asp?pr_id=5
[2011-05-29]

LEGO (2003). *Annual Report 2003.* [Online], Available:
http://cache.lego.com/upload/contentTemplating/AboutUsFactsAndFiguresContent/otherfiles/
download049677E7DF3EF6655CF3EE4ADF8DF598.pdf
[2011-03-10]

LEGO (2004). *Annual Report 2004.* [Online], Available:
http://cache.lego.com/upload/contentTemplating/AboutUsFactsAndFiguresContent/otherfiles/
downloadF838449F9632717923954190E3DE504A.pdf
[2011-03-12]

LEGO (2005). *Annual Report 2005.* [Online], Available:
http://cache.lego.com/upload/contentTemplating/AboutUsFactsAndFiguresContent/otherfiles/
download9FAE9DB028E150C8CAAF7D4CA51C6BBA.pdf
[2011-04-13]

LEGO (2006a). *Annual Report 2006.* [Online], Available:
http://cache.lego.com/upload/contentTemplating/AboutUsFactsAndFiguresContent/otherfiles/
download1D4EDD40D9A29DD8ADFFDABDD249C729.pdf
[2011-04-23]

LEGO (2007a). *Annual Report 2007.* [Online], Available:
http://cache.lego.com/upload/contentTemplating/AboutUsFactsAndFiguresContent/otherfiles/
downloadD1AC784E0C5E8AE82B2B003CD88C4464.pdf
[2011-03-15]

LEGO (2008a). *Annual Report 2008.* [Online], Available:
http://cache.lego.com/upload/contentTemplating/AboutUsFactsAndFiguresContent/otherfiles/
downloadF7A616C11EDF554703D451946115EB1A.pdf
[2011-04-17]

LEGO (2009a). *Annual Report 2009.* [Online], Available:
http://cache.lego.com/upload/contentTemplating/AboutUsFactsAndFiguresContent/otherfiles/
download786B425E6D7ED2B4EF0297D6423EC7ED.pdf
[2011-04-10]

LEGO (2010a). *Annual Report 2010.* [Online], Available:
http://cache.lego.com/upload/contentTemplating/AboutUsFactsAndFiguresContent/otherfiles/
downloadE994290D230BFB0E2A914F4DC3B6531C.pdf
[2011-04-10]

LEGO (2006b). *Sustainability Report 2006.* [Online], Available:
http://cache.lego.com/upload/contentTemplating/AboutUsCorporateResponsibilityCon
tent/otherfiles/download75BB477FDF379280E2D8B92AD0CF7F3D.pdf
[2011-05-18]

LEGO (2007b). *Sustainability Report 2007.* [Online], Available:
http://cache.lego.com/upload/contentTemplating/AboutUsCorporateResponsibilityCon
tent/otherfiles/download4D513A1A42B8F11CB4F291FED6FCB330.pdf
[2011-04-27]

LEGO (2008b). *Progress Report 2008.* [Online], Available:
http://cache.lego.com/upload/contentTemplating/AboutUsCorporateResponsibilityCon
tent/otherfiles/downloadF4473BCFA5049B745A162D8E5EEFE83D.pdf
[2011-04-15]

LEGO (2009b). *Progress Report 2009.* [Online], Available:
http://cache.lego.com/upload/contentTemplating/AboutUsCorporateResponsibilityCon
tent/otherfiles/download384F882F920FFD7ADCF6974F1D194AB0.pdf
[2011-04-30]

LEGO (2010b). *Progress Report 2010.* [Online], Available:
http://cache.lego.com/upload/contentTemplating/AboutUsCorporateResponsibilityCon
tent/otherfiles/downloadEF7733FE56DFDFBC57D0DED578F73612.pdf
[2011-04-21]

LEGO (2010c). *Company Profile 2010.* [Online]. Available:
http://cache.lego.com/upload/contentTemplating/AboutUsFactsAndFiguresContent/oth
erfiles/download98E142631E71927FDD52304C1C0F1685.pdf
[2011-05-11]

LEGO (2011a) *The LEGO Group increases its market share,* [press release]. March 3,
2011 Available:
http://aboutus.lego.com/enUS/pressroom/Default.aspx?y=276303&l=200071&n=5
[2011-05-71]

LEGO (2011b), 2011. *About us* [Electronic]. Available:
http://aboutus.lego.com/en-us/group/future.aspx
[2011-05-20]

Kaisen Different (2011). Building a LEGO world. [Electronic]. Available:
http://www.kaisen.co.uk/h2hautumn04/pdf/page2.pdf
[2011-05-29]

New Inventions Success, 2011 [Electronic]. Availble:
http://www.new-inventions-success.com/Innovation-Definition.html
[2011-05-02]

OHSAS (2010) *OHSAS 18001 website* Availble:
http://www.ohsas-18001-occupational-health-and-safety.com/
[2011-05-13]

Interview

Kundstorp, J. V., (2009) *Lessons from the crisis, finding light in the storm.* The 11th
Nikkei Global Management Forum. Interviewed by Dr. John R.Wells [video online],
26-27 Oct, Japan. Available:http://www.youtube.com/watch?v=-w6I51w4R60
[2011-06-02]

CPSIA information can be obtained at www.ICGtesting.com
Printed in the USA
LVOW051939070313

323223LV00001B/270/P